Don't Take It Personally

*New
Century
Books*

Don't Take It Personally

Race, Immigration, Crime and Other Heresies

Frank Borzellieri

New Century Foundation

Copyright © 2004 by New Century Foundation and Frank Borzellieri

All rights reserved, including the right to reproduce this book or parts thereof.

First Printing

New Century Books
Box 780142
Maspeth, New York 11378

www.culturalstudiespress.com
www.amren.com

Library of Congress Cataloging-in-Publication Data

Library of Congress Control Number: 2004109702

Borzellieri, Frank.
    Don't take it personally : race, immigration, crime and other heresies /
    Frank Borzellieri, Samuel Francis.
    Oakton, VA : New Century Foundation, 2004.
    p. cm.

    ISBN 0-9656383-3-2

Additional copies of this book may be ordered directly from the publisher.

Cover design by Rodney Jung
Cover photo by Photography by Asta

Manufactured in the United States of America

Dedicated to

Jamie Noelle Kocher

"They are equal unto the angels; and are the children of God." (Luke 20:36)

Acknowledgments

This book is a compilation of articles and essays, all of which required an extensive amount of research (except perhaps, for "When God Lived in New York," my column on the 1969 New York Mets, which I penned exclusively from memory.) The New Century Foundation, as always, was invaluable to me in my pursuit of the unspeakable truths about race.

So thanks to the man who wrote the foreword to my first book, Jared Taylor, for his relentless efforts in enlightening America on the most pressing issues of the day. Jared is the man whom *Newsday* dubbed my "most trusted mentor," which I liked because it reveals that he's older than me. He has been indispensable in the publishing of this book and is rightfully characterized as the leader of the Eurocentrist opposition.

Thanks also to the staff at New Century:

Stephen Webster, for all the effort he put into this book's publication, as well as for the research he did for his 2001 article, "Writing on the Wall," which eerily came out a month before September 11th.

Jim Lubinskas, for what had to be painful research in exploring the hip-hop magazine, "The Source." Also to Jim for his encouraging greetings whenever he sees me, saying "Jambo" instead of "hello," the well-known Swahili word taught to the illiterate students in the New York City school system. Funny, Jim.

And thanks to Roger McGrath for his stark immigration findings which I utilized in the article, "Reconquista." And to Jerry Levine for his work on the awful murders in Waco.

And George McDaniel for his promotion of all my books on the worldwide web.

Special thanks to Loretta ("Lora") Sanchez, the office manager at the Queens Ledger Newspaper Group, who often shook her head in despair upon seeing my weekly column and who graciously took all those phone calls from the public in support of me. Lora never tired of trying to change my mind and said I was most like a son to her in those times when I wouldn't listen to her -- which was most of the time. But she definitely made me more of an animal lover than I ever was, which, of course, means she made me a better person. The newspaper was known for its love and support of animals, and I was happy to be a part of it.

And thanks again to Walter Sanchez for happily publishing and totally agreeing with every word I ever wrote (just kidding.)

Special thanks to Sam Francis, a lion in the fight against multicultural madness, who wrote the foreword to this book.

Finally, thanks to my good friend and fellow Met fan, Peter Mannarino, who provided that great, old-fashioned, taped-up baseball bat, which I grip with pine tar on the cover of this book.

Contents

FOREWORD	1
INTRODUCTION	5
I *CULTURE*	11
Diallo Case About Race	13
O.J. Still Searching for Real Killer	15
The Politics of AIDS	18
Happy Kwanzaa	20
Kosovo Proves Diversity's a Weakness	23
The Fallacy of Environmental Racism	25
HIV: A Very Strange Civil Right	28
"Americans" With Foreign Loyalties	30
Was Jesus Homeless?	32
White Sports Mascots a Tradition	34
How to Deal With "The Sopranos"	37
The Source	40
AIDS: The Great White Plot	42

	Dr. Laura and the New Censorship	45
	The Problem With Islam	48
	The Assault on Fishing	50
	Was Cleopatra Black?	53
	Is Sex With Animals Normal?	55
	White Hypocrisy on Integration	58
	When God Lived in New York	61
II	*RACE AND GENETICS*	65
	For Whom the Bell Curve Tolls	67
	Heterodox: Nature Trumps Nurture	69
	Why It Matters	72
	No Quotas Needed in Sports	75
	Taboo: Why Blacks Dominate Sports	77
	Wanted: Black Organ Donors	80
	The Biological Reality of Race	83
III	*POLITICS AND GOVERNMENT*	87
	Race Commission Report a Farce	89
	What Head Start?	91

	Health Care: Government is the Problem	94
	Medicare, Medicaid and HMO's	96
	Court Tyranny a Liberal Creation	99
	The Ultimate Price of Quotas	101
	Wackos at Waco Finally Confess	104
	What Ashcroft Faced in Missouri	107
	The Only Legal Ponzi Scheme	110
	Who Wants to Be a Black Man?	112
IV	*CRIME AND GUN CONTROL*	117
	Finally: Truth on Race and Hate Crimes	119
	Race, Crime and Guns	121
	Abortion, Crime and Race	124
	The Million Nut March	126
	Massacre at Wendy's Thanks to Gun Control	129
	Put McGruff to Sleep	131
	Some "Hate Crimes" More Equal Than Others	134
	Kennesaw Embarrasses Gun Controllers	136
	Gun Buyback Program a Sham	139

	Racial Profiling is Justified	141
	The Church and the Death Penalty	144
	True Feminine Protection	147
	Racial Profiling Lives!	149
V	*PROFILES*	153
	Hide Your Guns From Schumer	155
	Blackmun: Death of a Despot	157
	Dinkins: Still a Loser	160
	Culbert the Victim of Thought Police	163
	Until We Meet Again, Jamie	166
VI	*IMMIGRATION*	169
	The Coming Dark Age	171
	Wretched Refuse a Health Hazard	173
	Reconquista	176
	Cardinal Sins on Immigration	178
	Immigration Policy Proves Deadly	181
	U.S. Law Welcomes Terrorists	184
ABOUT THE AUTHOR		189

Foreword

by Samuel Francis

Not long after being fired from *The Washington Times* in 1995, ostensibly for expressing what might be called "Racially Incorrect" opinions, I founded a fictitious organization known as the Association of Fired Journalists—the AFJ. In order to join the AFJ, you have to have been fired as a journalist for expressing *verboten* thoughts. Janet Cooke and Jayson Blair are not eligible; being fired for plagiarism doesn't count as a qualification, nor does being fired for incompetence, beating the daylights out of your editor, or not being able to spell correctly — you have to have been fired because of the opinions you've expressed or the facts you've reported — that's all.

Well, there's one other condition also, though it's not in the by-laws: Communists, liberals, and Europhobes can't get in. The only journalists we recognize as martyrs are people like ourselves, guys (or girls) who get dumped because what they said or wrote violates the dogmas that the communists, liberals, and Europhobes have imposed.

At first, I was the only member of the AFJ, but I soon noticed it was a growing and increasingly distinguished body. Its First Vice President is Joe Sobran, who got the bounce from *National Review*, also for expressing opinions that are *verboten*. Then there's Scott McConnell, now executive editor of Pat Buchanan's *The American Conservative*, but before that fired as editorial page editor at the *New York Post* after writing a perfectly sensible editorial opposing statehood for Puerto Rico. The Puerto Ricans didn't like it, mobbed the paper, and demanded his head. The intrepid management quickly obliged.

Also there's Peter Brimelow, another senior editor of *National Review*, who is probably the leading critic of immigration in the country, author of *Alien Nation*, a widely praised study of the effects of mass immigration, and a senior editor of *Forbes* as well as *National Review*, in addition to being the founding webmaster of Vdare.com, a website devoted entirely to immigration and the "national question." Peter joined the AFJ when William F. Buckley Jr. decided that running his pieces criticizing immigration didn't fit the agenda of the Rainbow Republicanism that Newt Gingrich, Bill Kristol, Linda Chavez, and other heavyweights were pushing and which Buckley wanted *National Review* to parrot.

There are other members of the Association of Fired Journalists as well, but I trust the reader gets the picture.

Sadly, I am forced to report that Frank Borzellieri is not and never has been a member of the Association, though I also have to confess that I am puzzled as to why he isn't.

"Sadly," I say, because I'd love to have Frank join the rest of our prestigious but impoverished band at our annual (and also fictitious) conventions, but the reason he hasn't joined is that, for reasons entirely unknown to me, he just hasn't been fired — yet.

Why he hasn't been fired I can't possibly tell you. Maybe it's because, as he argues in his introduction to this book, he has the support of an increasingly rare breed in American journalism — an honest and courageous editor. If so, Frank is luckier than all the other members of the AFJ combined as well as just about every other journalist in the country.

Nevertheless, Frank has done nearly everything he can think of to make himself eligible to join the AFJ — he writes about race and intelligence, for example, and actually tells the truth about it. Also a few reflections on such subjects as immigration, multiculturalism, gun control, homosexuality, abortion, feminism and women, and a good many others, all from a decidedly incorrect point of view. And he writes ably, often powerfully, and accurately. He even spells correctly (usually). So I have no idea why he hasn't been fired.

You can catch the flavor of Frank's writing and the seriousness of the problem as to why he hasn't been canned by taking just one excerpt from one column republished here, a column entitled "Racial Profiling Is Justified." I'll bet you're already getting the drift. Frank writes,

> "In the case of racial profiling, the crusade to eliminate it is not merely the province if liberals. In fact, there is not one conservative politician in America who would defend it. There are no police departments that admit to practicing it or would defend it if it was found to be permeating their officers' tactics. Unlike affirmative action or racial set-asides, there are not two *public* sides to racial profiling. *Everyone* says it's wrong and *everyone* states that it must be ended."

"Everyone" except Frank, of course.

Frank Borzellieri has made it his business to defend the indefensible. Liberals love to crow about the late William Kunstler, who defended the black mass murderer of whites Colin Ferguson, killer of several whites on a New York train some years ago, as a defender of the indefensible, but the truth is that most of the causes "crusaders" like Kunstler or Alan Dershowitz or other professional and celebrated crusaders take up are perfectly fashionable and safe. When was the last time you heard of a journalist being fired for defending the Scottsboro Boys or for denouncing American society as "racist"?

The people who get fired, who get punished or muzzled, are not those on the political left. They are people on the political right. There is a simple but largely unacknowledged reason for that. The reason is that it is the left in our culture that is dominant, that controls what is said and how it is said, and not the right at all. The right — especially if it is a real right and not a phony right that at bottom is indistinguishable from the left — is the real opposition in American society, politics, and culture. It is the left that runs the place, makes the rules, and enforces them.

In recent years, there has been a mass reaction to the hegemony of the left, manifested most clearly in institutions like talk radio, but also in all kinds of alternative media — the Internet especially (check out Vdare.com, for instance), but also in newsletters like Jared Taylor's *American Renaissance*, full-scale newspapers like the *Citizens Informer* (of which I have the honor to be editor) and *Middle American News*, and organizations like the Council of Conservative Citizens and countless dinner clubs, discussion groups, neighborhood associations, and other informal grassroots organizations that are starting to notice certain unpleasant and frightening truths about our country.

They notice that neither side in the debates on television or their local newspapers really disagrees with each other on the issues they care about (which happen to be the issues that guys like Frank, I, and the other members of the AFJ write about all the time). They notice that on such issues as racial profiling, race itself, immigration, and multiculturalism almost no one in the establishment media (that is, the media controlled by the left) takes an opposing position. And they are beginning to notice that some people — definitely not in the establishment media — do take an opposing position on these and similar issues.

The real hope for what is left of American society, the American nation, and the civilization we have created in this country lies precisely in writers like Frank Borzellieri, because they are the only guys in the country who are willing to tell truths the left-wing media don't want you to hear and won't let you hear. They are also the only guys who are able to tell it, accurately and fairly, without a lot of silliness, wacky speculation, and unreliable reporting.

And what that means is that as more and more Americans realize that it's the Frank Borzellieris of the world who are telling them stuff no one else will let them hear, they will increasingly turn to guys like Frank to get those truths.

Which is why it's so amazing he hasn't been fired already.

Sooner or later, however, I fully expect Frank to be eligible for membership in the Association of Fired Journalists. It's simply an oversight on the part of the management that he hasn't been bounced off his column already. But until he is, he needs to keep writing what he offers in this book and the columns it contains, and you, dear readers, need to keep reading him and giving him your support.

Introduction

The very first book I ever read in my life was at age nine. I'm not referring to a children's book, or reading that was required in school. I mean the first *real* book – an adult's book, a best-seller. And of course, the book concerned the most important thing in the life of most nine year-olds – baseball. But this was no ordinary baseball book. It was not a biography of some Hall of Famer; not a history of the game; and not an instructional "how to" book. No, this was the book which New York Public Library recently included on its list of the One Hundred most influential books of the Twentieth Century.

The book was "Ball Four" and the author Jim Bouton.

Bouton had been a solid pitcher with the New York Yankees and, after arm trouble, was traded away. "Ball Four" was Bouton's personal diary and observations of the 1969 season, which he spent with the Seattle Pilots and the Houston Astros. It was the original "behind the scenes" and "tell all" book. These types of book are so common today that it is difficult for people to understand what a bombshell Bouton had unleashed when the book was released in 1970. It simply had never been done before. Bouton had exposed publicly what in those days was only known privately about the drunkenness, sexual exploits and outrageous behavior of so many of America's heroes. Mickey Mantle would not speak to Bouton for years. Bouton was banned from Old-timers reunions at Yankee Stadium. Baseball Commissioner Bowie Kuhn tried to force Bouton to sign a statement claiming that the revelations in the book were untrue.

Simply put, to say that Bouton was a controversial figure would be a gross understatement.

The reaction to "Ball Four" was unbelievable in its ferocity. Soon after his retirement in the early 70's, Bouton took a job at Channel 7, the ABC affiliate in New York, as a sports broadcaster for the top-rated Eyewitness News. Bouton was just as sarcastic and funny on television as he had been in "Ball Four." Although his politics – though not relevant — were certainly to the left, I was an enormous fan of Bouton's.

It was during those days as a sportscaster that Bouton wrote the sequel to "Ball Four." Although it told the story of Bouton's television work, it was basically a book about the *reaction* to "Ball Four." And man, was there fallout.

The title of that book was "I'm Glad You Didn't Take It Personally." And so the title of this book – my own sequel to "The Unspoken Truth" – is a take on Bouton's sequel to "Ball Four."

There are more differences than similarities between Bouton's books and mine. First of all, "The Unspoken Truth" was not about baseball. It was, for the most part, not written in the first person. It was not really a personal account, and it was not a "behind the scenes" tome. So the title of this book is more of a tribute to Bouton and "Ball Four" and my personal experience and enjoyment of his books than anything else.

Still, there are similarities. Both books created a whirlwind of controversy within their own orbits. Bouton and I were both reviled for writing the truth. Both of us were persona non grata in certain circles. And both of us have stories to tell regarding the reaction to our work.

When "The Unspoken Truth" was released, *Newsday* wrote that I was the man "with a sharp tongue and a sharper pen."

Walter Sanchez, the owner and publisher of the Ledger-Observer newspaper chain that published my columns, has his own stories of anxiety to tell about carrying my column. In fact, it was Walter much more than me that had to stand up to the Thought Police and other voices of intolerance who wanted me fired and censored. In one instance, he relented. After I penned a diatribe against a New York City Board of Education official who happened to be a friend of Walter's, my column was suspended for nine weeks. Walter, who came under enormous pressure to sack me, was in this instance of course, wrong. But to his credit, he printed full pages of letters to the editor demanding my reinstatement. The letters, which ran eight to one in my favor, were often highly critical of him. He could have thrown them away and the public would not have been any the wiser.

Still, he printed them, publicly stating that he was giving the public what it wanted – a conservative Eurocentric voice that they could not find in another mainstream publication.

The entire incident of my suspension became citywide news, with the *New York Times* running front page stories more than once until I was reinstated.

Hostility toward a Eurocentrist writer who deals openly on matters of race did not begin with me. Sam Francis, the most gifted columnist in America and the man who has written the Foreword to this book, was fired not once, but twice, by the *Washington Times* for writing and speaking honestly about race. Sam once joked with me that you haven't really arrived as a columnist until you've been suspended for gross political incorrectness.

And the invective one receives as a right-wing columnist actually says much more about my detractors than it says about me. One of the most unattractive qualities (and there are many, Lord knows) possessed by liberals is there propensity for personal attacks simply because they disagree. Jared Taylor has pointed out that those who take a Eurocentric view on race are not merely regarded by liberals as wrong, but as *evil*. Indeed, George Will has said, "Disagree with a with a conservative and he'll call you dense. Disagree with a liberal and he'll call you lacking in goodness and compassion."

But there's more to it than that. We all know people who never compliment other people. No matter the circumstances, they simply cannot say a flattering thing to another person. Now, every first year psychology student knows that people like that are so lacking in self-confidence that they feel threatened to even have to acknowledge the positive qualities or accomplishments of others. This reasoning also applies to liberals and their methods.

So many liberals will always say the most vile things about those with whom they disagree. And they make it personal. They can never simply acknowledge an honest disagreement. They must always inject personal attacks into their response. This betrays an extreme lack of confidence in their own beliefs. People secure in their own arguments would merely state them — secure in the knowledge that the facts and the evidence would bear them out. But deep down, liberals – so filled with rage at their lack of a coherent argument – resort to name-calling. So lacking in confidence, so empty of any intellectual capacity, they fall back on accusations of bigotry – today's version of the last refuge of a scoundrel.

I had written a column blasting the Catholic Church as hopelessly liberal on social policy and on the hierarchy's opposition to the death penalty (see "The Church and the Death Penalty" page 144.) In response to this column, a letter to the editor was received and published from a Timothy Pasek. Not only was Mr. Pasek a Catholic priest, he was the pastor of a huge Catholic flock in Queens, New York. Although I had never heard of him, people told me that he was very well-liked by his congregation.

So here was a man, given his background, schooling and training, who almost by definition had to know more about Catholicism than me. He certainly would be possessed of impressive ammunition in debating me. If nothing else, this would be a genuine intellectual debate of vigor.

Forget it. Mr. Pasek's letter began, "I realize you [the editor] are not responsible for the views of a certain person by the name of Frank Borzellieri." This was his way, I guess, of offering Walter Sanchez absolution for what other clergy might consider the sin of publishing me. The rest of the letter, a vacuous meandering diatribe, asserted that my views made him "want to regurgitate."

I did not respond to this letter publicly, but it undoubtedly did Mr. Pasek more harm than good. Not only was such vitriol unbecoming a priest, it totally lacked any intellectual thrust and relevant citations. His tirade was indistinguishable from the other fanatics I was confronted with weekly.

(I refer to him as "Mr." Pasek rather than "Father" because about a year later, a news story broke all over the New York television and print news about a pastor in Queens who ran away abruptly from his parish to Arizona, told no one, married his secretary, and was now living in there. He was, of course, defrocked. Yes, this was the same Defender of the Faith, Timothy Pasek. Hey, at least he ran away with a grown woman, not a little boy!)

But the larger point is that this simply demonstrates how liberals behave when faced with a dissenting point of view that they cannot hope to counter on the merits.

And so this brings us to the matter of race, and writings on race and intelligence. The job of a columnist is (or at least is supposed to be) not only to give opinions, but to stir things up a bit, to break ground all others are afraid to break. The reason my column stood out as it did, and actually made "news" in other publications, including competitors, is because I crossed the uncrossable line created by today's elite intelligentsia. It was so common that it became cliché that people would tell me they agreed with me privately, but would express wide-eyed astonishment that such views were actually printed in a mainstream newspaper that endorsed Chuck Schumer for United States Senate. And once again, the credit goes to the publisher Walter Sanchez.

It was not always smooth sailing with Walter. After the first two columns in a three-part series on race and intelligence (see page 67), Walter called me into his office. "Don't you realize I have a family to feed?" he said. It seems that some black hotshot bank executive threatened to pull advertising as retribution for the columns. The problem was that part three was due to be published in the next issue, and the readership was expecting it. Walter demanded to see this third installment before we went to press. But, alas, he printed it exactly as I wrote it. In his own way, and without realizing it, Walter Sanchez, a moderate Democrat, was a trailblazer in mainstream newspaper publishing.

The writings in this book received quite a reaction when they first appeared. Compiling them in a collection opens them up to a whole new audience (and to liberal reviewers who will cringe, yet again.) I challenge them all not to take it personally, but to attempt to refute my arguments using intelligent reasoning – a quality liberals sorely lack.

And for those who look forward to reading the truth about the most controversial issues of our time, you've come to the right place.

I
CULTURE

Diallo Case About Race

News accounts and other assorted variations of punditry and commentary on the Amadou Diallo case invariably describe the matter as an issue of police brutality. Some others refer to the case as a referendum on the mayoralty of Rudy Giuliani. Indeed, defenders of the police and the Mayor have fallen all over themselves citing significantly reduced crime rates — especially in minority areas — and pulling out statistics proving that the New York City police force is among the most restrained in the country.

All of these people are wasting their time. The Diallo case is about race.

Certainly, the protesters at One Police Plaza, and now Washington, are yelping about alleged mistreatment on the part of police, but the crux of their complaint is brutality *as it applies to race.* None of these protesters would be marching if Diallo had been an orthodox Jew.

Furthermore, none of the Mayor's defenders can possibly believe that the protesters are interested in reason. It is a preposterous, even hilarious notion that the protesters will actually take the time to examine or even acknowledge the fact that crime has been significantly thwarted in non-white areas of New York City. Facts do not interest them. They are vicious and they want blood.

In fact, the only ones who are in any way being honest about their motivations are the black protesters themselves. "Whites have been getting away with violence against people of color for years," one woman remarked. The fact that this is untrue is almost beside the point. What does matter is not violence against blacks, as she sees it, but violence against blacks committed by whites. The placards depicting Giuliani as Hitler and the signs equating the NYPD with the KKK are sufficient evidence as to the degenerate character of the marchers, which have clearly established Al Sharpton as the most powerful black man in New York.

Again, it would be a waste of time trying to appeal to an angry mob to face reality. Blacks commit most of the violent crime in

America today. This has always been the case. They are ten times as likely to commit a crime of violence as whites. And when whites do commit violence, they choose a black victim only 2.4 percent of the time. Blacks choose a white victim more than half the time. So what these numbers actually reveal in addition to the obvious — that blacks are inveterately more violent than whites — is that there is actually more black on white crime than black on black crime.

If any group, therefore, had the moral imperative backed up by indisputable evidence to protest its victimization, it is whites who should be protesting the violence they have been subjected to by blacks, not the other way around. So where are the white protesters? Yeah, right.

On the matter of the different standard with which police treat the different races, hardly a new allegation, the radical anarchists would argue that it is police racism that accounts for the difference. But police statistics reveal that minority officers are rougher with non-whites than white officers. And the average cop will point out matter-of-factly that if blacks are treated differently by police it is simply because they are the ones committing most of the crimes.

Of course, it is entirely possible that Giuliani's defenders are hauling out the crime stats for the consumption of the public at large in order to boost his political standing, not in the deluded belief that the protesters can be reasoned with. But the public already knows the truth. The police and the Mayor would do better to trot out the racial crime statistics and ask the protesters to explain them. It would, at least, make for great theater.

The protesters, even without Sharpton, can only be described as an urban rogues gallery of low-lives, degenerates and squalid hoodlums who emanate from the bowels of New York's particularly disgusting race politics. They include Congressmen Charles Rangel and Eliot Engel and New York's former mayor, David Dinkins, whose claim to fame (besides being the most inept mayor in the City's history) is his tolerance of the Crown Heights pogrom and the Korean boycott — both stark episodes of black criminality. As a side, but motivating issue, the protesters have never forgiven Giuliani for defeating him. The whites who have joined in the protests, including starlet Susan Sarandon, blend right in.

The fact that Amadou Diallo was an African, not an American, proves that the protesters are informed by race and not justice. Diallo left Africa of his own free will to immigrate to the United States, rather than choose another African country. He should not be reproached for making such a rational choice — so rational that he had to believe that the promise of justice in America was greater than anywhere else.

Now he has become a racial symbol for a problem that doesn't exist — police brutality — and a lightning rod for racial arsonists who, deep down, couldn't care less about him and are overjoyed that he has provided them with the opportunity to set New York City on fire.

O.J. Still Searching For Real Killer

Three years ago this week, after languishing in prison for fourteen months, O.J. Simpson was finally set free by a jury which was determined — in the interests of racial solidarity — to acquit the man who slit his wife's throat from ear to ear, nearly decapitating her.

At the time of this travesty, during a post-verdict press conference, the inept District Attorney Gil Garcetti managed to crack a half-smile when a reporter queried as to whether this would trigger another search for the killer. "Just because there has been a not guilty verdict doesn't mean we have the wrong man," he said. The task, it seemed, would be left to O.J. Simpson himself, who volunteered that he would indeed find the "real killer." He has probably undertaken this endeavor when the cameras are off, and in between golf matches.

The verdict in the Simpson case, widely predicted by whites without blinders on, was the most profound and significant reality check in the history of race relations in America, the equivalent of an anvil landing on the heads of naive whites. For some, the moment of the verdict resulted in a first-time eye-opening experience which forever shattered silly illusions about racial realities. Other whites, literally, cried or became physically ill. Still others were visibly chilled and shaken at the sight of all those black hoodlum law students at Howard University erupting in wild cheers and celebration. Whites finally realized, despite those nonsensical polls which showed a majority of blacks believing O.J. to be innocent, that the real reason blacks were jubilant was not because they *really* believed their man was not guilty, but because they knew that their hero murderer was guilty and were overjoyed that he had gotten away with it.

The establishment made heroic efforts to hammer home the point that the "legal system" failed, but in reality it was the concept of multi-racialism that failed. Whatever mistakes the prosecution may have made, the reason O.J. Simpson was acquitted, in the face of such obvious and overwhelming evidence of guilt, was because the blacks on the jury had a "score to settle." Minutes after one juror (a former black panther) gave O.J. the black power salute, prosecutor Christopher Darden nearly collapsed at the press conference, sobbing in mid-sentence. Months later, Darden would say, "On the first day of trial, I looked into those faces on the jury and I knew what was coming."

Indeed, Darden was called every variation of "Uncle Tom" and needed to hire bodyguards because of the threats against his life. Prosecutor Marcia Clark said, "A majority black jury won't convict in a case like this. They won't bring justice." Darden's father had told him the same thing.

In addition to the degenerate law pupils, students at historically black Morehouse College in Atlanta erupted in delirious pandemonium following the verdict. On New York City's subways, black teenagers were chanting, "Not guilty, not guilty." One teen was observed saying, "Now he's free and will assassinate someone else." "Assassinate" is a quite telling term — signifying that many blacks consider themselves to be in a permanent state of war against whites. In Los Angeles, gangs covered walls with the message, "O.J., you owe us your life," referring to the fact that the threat of riots may have assisted in the verdict.

The swine defense attorney Johnnie Cochran said before the trial if he had one black, he'd deliver a hung jury; if he had five, he'd get an acquittal. The District Attorney gave him ten.

Some apologists for the jury tried to make the point that a "not guilty" verdict merely means the jury could not determine guilt beyond a reasonable doubt (as if there were any doubt), not that they necessarily believed Simpson to be innocent. But that's not what the jurors themselves said. One dismissed juror asserted that the prosecution had "a whole lotta nothin'." Juror Brenda Moran said, "We don't know who killed her. But we know O.J. Simpson didn't."

Blacks have shown with remarkable consistency and durability throughout the years that evidence and justice are barely considerations at all compared to racial consciousness. The late Bronx District Attorney Mario Merola remarked as far back as the late 1970's that it was virtually impossible to get black juries to convict other blacks who had victimized whites.

But the Simpson case provided Americans, for the first time, with this startling reality right in their living rooms. Never before had the country seen exactly what was presented as evidence before a jury in a spectacular trial. The unbridgeable chasm between the white and black worlds — where both races look at the same thing and see something so entirely different — was revealed nakedly.

The silver lining in this tragedy is that the Simpson trial acted as a catalyst for a white awakening of sorts. A Eurocentric publication polled its subscribers in 1996, with one of the questions being, "What Americans have most advanced white interests?" O.J. Simpson made the list of finalists.

So now with O.J. still searching for the real killer, blacks remain jubilant that their man is free. Whites are sadder... but wiser.

The Politics of AIDS

The announcement of the extraordinary decline of AIDS as a major health scourge in America has translated, quite predictably, into very bad news for the radical homosexual lobby. Just as "civil rights" leaders have always denied progress and insisted "not much has changed," so too did AIDS activists twist themselves into red ribbons last week trying to explain away the emerging facts about the only politicized disease in American history.

After years of wildly hysterical claims that AIDS was a disease destined to be the new Black Plague, already breaking out into the general population affecting "everyone," it was revealed by the federal government that AIDS deaths fell an astounding 50 percent since last year. That figure represents the biggest decline ever (15,000 fewer deaths) for a major cause of death in one year. AIDS dropped from eighth to fourteenth place, the first time it has not placed in the top ten in a decade. Terrible news for the lobbyists so successful at extorting dollars from the American taxpayer in order to underwrite their own depraved behavior.

The history of the HIV/AIDS epidemic would actually be quite amusing if it concerned anything other than a horrible deadly disease. It is as much a *political* history as it is a medical history. When AIDS first reared its ugly head in the early 1980's, it soon gained a reputation as the "gay disease." The homosexual lobby labored tirelessly to try and portray AIDS as "everyone's disease," focusing on the rare instances of contraction through blood transfusions. Through massive propaganda and the assistance of the media, AIDS activists were largely successful in this endeavor.

The reason it was necessary to pretend AIDS was a disease like any other, able to strike any segment of the general population, was for funding purposes. It was understood that the American public would never support massive amounts of tax dollars being poured into the coffers of a disease which was almost exclusively the province of homosexuals and intravenous drug users. More significantly, radical AIDS activists knew Americans would be further reluctant knowing that it was the grossly irresponsible and perverse behavior of those groups that was spreading the disease.

Despite the propaganda campaign and the wild predictions of millions dead (including a warning by Oprah Winfrey that by 1990, 20 percent of the American heterosexual population would be dead from AIDS), the disease never "broke out" into the general population. By the early 1990's the epidemic, in fact, leveled off. It became clear that AIDS turned out to be the "gay disease" everyone originally thought it was.

The Center for Disease Control reported several years ago that two-thirds of AIDS cases worldwide were caused by homosexual or bisexual males. Another 17 percent were caused by intravenous drug users. Only four percent were classified as heterosexual. And even that figure was deceptively high, with half of that classification having heterosexual contact with a person with AIDS and the other half assumed to be "heterosexual" because the transmission occurred in places like Haiti and Central Africa, where heterosexual transmission is assumed to play a major role.

Notwithstanding these facts, the politics of AIDS knows no bounds. Since the beginning of the epidemic, AIDS has taken less than 200,000 lives. But 40,000 women die of breast cancer *every year*. More than a million Americans are diagnosed with cancer yearly, with half dying from it. Three quarters of a million people will die of heart disease yearly. Yet AIDS receives the most funding while killing far less. On top of this, AIDS activists are constantly bellowing that yet *more* money is needed.

Anyone with an honest grasp of the numbers, therefore, would be somewhat less shocked at the most recent encouraging news. But the homosexual mouthpieces would have none of it. Since good news translates into less dollars, the remarkable drop in the death toll was met with hostility and tortured logic. Helene Gayle of the National Center for HIV, Sexually Transmitted Diseases and Tuberculosis Prevention warns that less deaths and people living longer, more normal lives with HIV means they are remaining alive to infect others. In other words, it would be better if those people simply got sick and died. Tacit in her logic is the admission that HIV-infected people will continue to behave irresponsibly and continue the same lifestyle which got them the disease in the first place.

Despite the propaganda charade that has become such big business in the lunatic world of AIDS politics, the facts are there for all to see. But what will they do now with all those red ribbons, anyway?

Happy Kwanzaa

Kwanzaa, which is described in the almanac as "an African-American celebration of family and black culture," is for the most part a mystery to the majority of Americans. Most people have a vague understanding of Kwanzaa, believing it to be some sort of black religious holiday which falls around Christmas. Other than that, the annual event remains obscure to whites, with very little comprehension as to what it really is and how it came about.

On the surface, the hoopla over Kwanzaa appears to be silly but relatively harmless (on the order of Black History Month) — a way of giving blacks a separate holiday to enjoy while everyone else is celebrating Christmas. Now, when people say "Happy Holidays," the politically correct go out of their way to include Kwanzaa in this message. Yes, Bill Clinton's White House now issues Kwanzaa greetings.

Kwanzaa, which in Swahili means "first fruit of the harvest," was invented in 1966 by Ron Karenga (who now goes by the name "Maulana"), then a graduate student, now the chairman of the Black Studies Department at the University of California at Long Beach. Karenga's inspiration for what he terms this "political act of self-determination" was the Watts riots.

The holiday is actually a seven-day event beginning on December 26, with each day extolling a different African principle. Commonly known as the "seven principles of Kwanzaa," but perhaps more appropriately described as the Seven Days of Socialism, the principles are: umaja (unity); kujichagulia (self-determination); ujima (collective work and responsibility); ujamaa (cooperative economics); nia (purpose); kuumba (creativity); and imani (faith).

Families are expected to gather in the evening to celebrate the day's principle, light a black, red or green candle and place it in a seven-branched candleholder called a "kinara," which is supposed to give light to the principle. On the final day of Kwanzaa, the entire community joins together for a feast called the "karamu," with all participants adorned in African garb.

Last year, roughly 13 million American blacks are estimated to have spent $500 million celebrating Kwanzaa. Hallmark, which began selling Kwanzaa cards in 1992, now offers eleven different varieties. The National Museum of American History in Washington has put on a display called "Traditions of Christmas, Hanukkah, Kwanzaa and the New Year." In New York City, the American Museum of Natural History celebrates with an African Marketplace, poetry, folk tales and music. Likewise in Chicago, where the Ujamaa Family, a black self-help group, holds an African Market. Pepsi-Cola, Anheuser-Busch, Revlon, Chemical Bank, AT&T, and Time-Life Books have all paid for booths at Kwanzaa conventions. Outside the United States, Kwanzaa is observed by some 10 million people in Africa, Canada, the Caribbean and parts of Europe.

In his Kwanzaa greeting last year, Clinton said, "Today, we have a renewed sense of hope in America, a hope based on the idea that our great diversity can unite — not divide — our society."

Yeah, well, that's not exactly what the typical Kwanzaa celebrant has in mind. This "great diversity" notion continues to be solely the province of foolish whites. Blacks have no such illusions that Kwanzaa is intended to unite the different races and ethnicities that comprise America. The "unity" of which Kwanzaa speaks is the unity of black people only. Kwanzaa is, quite simply, a black separatist phenomenon. And Kwanzaa organizers, to their credit, do not pretend otherwise. They cannot be blamed for Bill Clinton's idiocy.

At a Kwanzaa celebration at the Roxbury Boys and Girls Club in Boston, a white mother of a mulatto child was asked by organizers to leave. "We've had a tradition of it being an all-African event for people of color," said Sadiki Kambon. When Harlem Ben & Jerry's workers at the Kwanzaa festival at the Jacob Javits Convention Center prayed for people to buy ice cream, some black celebrants decried such commercialism. But Cedric McClester, the festival spokesman, reassured the worriers that money-making is just fine, as long as it is blacks who make the profits.

None of this should come as any surprise to those who have taken the time to examine Kwanzaa for what it is and for what it purports to be. Although Kwanzaa was created in America by an American, its *raison d'etre* has very little use for the United States, other than to support American blacks. The main symbol of Kwanzaa is the black national flag, which is composed of three horizontal bars — red, black and green.

Melanet, a black organization which promotes Kwanzaa, explains, "Red, Black and Green are the oldest national colors known to man. They are used as the flag of the Black Liberation Movement in America today, but actually go back to the Zinj Empires of Ancient Africa, which existed thousands of years before Rome, Greece, France, England or America."

Now Melanet (which to an alliterate ear sounds very much like "melanin," the pigmentation in blacks' skin which Afro-centrists claim makes blacks superior to whites) goes on, "The Red, or the blood, stands as the top of all things. We lost our land through blood; and we cannot gain it except through blood... The Black man in this hemisphere has yet to obtain land which is represented by the Green. The acquisition of this land is the highest and noblest aspiration for the Black man on this continent, since without land there can be no freedom, justice, independence or equality."

Translated, this means the impetus for Kwanzaa is the violent insurrection by blacks for liberation and justice on what will be the former United States. It is symptomatic of blacks' alienation and separateness from American society and Western culture, needing to celebrate African principles at Christmas even though 90 percent of American blacks are Christians.

All that aside, Happy Kwanzaa.

Kosovo Proves Diversity's a Weakness

American military forces are at war and American lives are at risk. Tens of thousands of ethnic Albanians have been made refugees in their own country. People who owned homes and had careers are now homeless and jobless. Men have been rounded up and shot. Women have been tortured and raped. Hatreds that have existed for hundreds of years have flared up, although they had never really diminished. A decade ago in the same territory, before the tables were turned, the Serbians were made refugees. Accusations of atrocities and crimes against humanity have been leveled. Human misery on an inhuman scale is growing, and the scenes are shocking Americans as they view them on television.

All of these things are happening because of ethnic diversity — the same diversity which is constantly defined as a "strength." If there is one thing that both the Albanians and the Serbians would agree on, it is that diversity is certainly not a "strength." They would also agree that the statement, "diversity is a strength," which is beaten into the heads of Americans at every conceivable opportunity, is a concept so ridiculous that only gullible fools could be made to believe it.

The trick is not in explaining why diversity is a weakness, a hindrance, a burden and a constant source of conflict. That is the easy part. Explaining why diversity is undesirable is like explaining why an invasion of locusts is undesirable. The trick is to try and comprehend how anyone capable of human thought could possibly believe it to be a strength.

Not only in Kosovo, but throughout the world today, diversity of race, tribe, language or religion is the single main reason why people slaughter each other on a large scale. Whether in Northern Ireland, Bosnia, the Middle East or Western Africa, diversity existing in the same geographic territory is a source of great strife and intractable blood-letting. The Sikhs fighting in the Punjab want to break away from India. The Tamils want to break from Sri Lanka. The Ethiopian provinces of Tigre and Eretria also want the same. The people involved in all these conflicts would scoff at the idea that their differences are neutral and meaningless, let alone a "strength."

The conflict in Kosovo is between people who are both of the Caucasian race. In fact, most of the discord around the world is over differences not as salient as race. Conflicts exist because of less important differences such as religion. Race, of course, is the greatest cause of antipathy between groups because, unlike language or religion, it cannot change. But what Kosovo and Northern Ireland prove is that even people who are culturally similar cannot get along.

Peter Brimelow, in his book "Alien Nation," referred to Yugoslavia when making the point that massive immigration was destroying the United States as a nation. "The former Yugoslavs are fighting *despite* the fact that they are all the same race (white). Indeed, they are all members of the same general ethnic group (South Slav). Even the language spoken by the two major contestants (Serbs and Croats) is basically the same... *And that's the point.* Those minor differences were still enough to tear the country apart."

Shortly after the NATO involvement in Kosovo began, Bill Clinton went on national television and told Dan Rather how heartbroken he was over the matter that has "bedeviled" human beings since the beginning of time — that people who are different from each other have a hard time getting along. Finally!

The man who claims to glory in diversity and who has preached that it is a source of great strength has at last admitted that maybe it's not such a strength after all.

In 1996, Clinton said, "The expedition that Columbus... began more than 500 years ago, continues today as we experience and celebrate the vibrant influences of varied civilizations, not only from Europe, but also from around the world. America is stronger because of this diversity, and the democracy we cherish flourishes in the great mosaic we have created since 1492." He also told an Australian audience, "And, yes, we can prove that free societies can embrace the economic and social changes, and the ethnic, racial and religious diversity this new era brings and come out stronger and freer than ever." Imagine such a speech being given today in Kosovo. The combatants would call a cease-fire just to stop laughing.

The fact is that human nature has been stubbornly consistent. People simply prefer and get along better with other people like themselves. In fact, it is the groups that have the most contact with each other that most dislike each other. That is why there are race riots in American cities and campus upheavals on American universities. A *New York Times* headline recently, although probably unintentionally, captured the true results of diversity. It read, "Ethnic Feuding Divides Parade for Harmony."

The Fallacy of "Environmental Racism"

Since policy in America is rarely driven by facts and common sense, but rather by hysteria and nonsense, it is not surprising that cries of racism actually threaten to drive environmental policy. One of the more nutty concepts that has recently resurfaced goes by the name of "environmental racism," which is defined as the deliberate placing of landfills, waste dumps or pollution-causing structures in nonwhite neighborhoods.

"Environmental racism," which also goes by such colorful names as "toxic racism," "radioactive colonialism," and "garbage imperialism," is a charge that blends right into the racial madness that defines 1990's America. It holds that governments and private firms regulated by government simply view the lives of whites as more valuable and, therefore, willfully subject nonwhites to the dangers of exposure to environmental hazards. It is said, according to the theory, that nonwhites suffer disproportionately from cancer, respiratory illnesses and other health problems because of the presence of these facilities.

This phenomenon has entered the news recently because of a petition filed last year with the Environmental Protection Agency by Congressman Jose Serrano of the Bronx, in which he maintains that the presence of solid-waste transfer stations in the mostly-minority borough is racial discrimination. Predictably, the Clinton Administration has bought into this "garbage" and the White House Council of Environmental Quality, as well as the Justice Department, have announced a broad investigation into this alleged "civil rights" violation.

Sadly, in the minds of nonwhite radicals and hustlers, there is every reason to level these charges since they understand that shouts of racism, no matter how scurrilous and unfounded, effectively silence and intimidate whites in power. Neither the federal government nor other proponents of "environmental justice" have attempted to explain the presence of the Fresh Kills landfill on Staten Island, a borough whose population is 80 percent white.

If indeed, however, toxic chemical sites are more prevalent in nonwhite areas it would undoubtedly be for economic reasons that have no connection to race. When cities look for locales to place incinerators, they invariably look for neighborhoods with lower real estate values, making the enterprise a less expensive one. Since nonwhites have less money than whites, it would stand to reason that waste sites would be more prevalent in minority areas.

Alas, this is not the case. A 1987 report by the United Church of Christ, Commission for Racial Justice, undertaken for the purpose of proving the "environmental racism" theory, found that 78 percent of hazardous waste landfills were located in areas with more white residents than nonwhites. It also found that 57 percent of blacks and Hispanics live near toxic waste sites, while 54 percent of whites do — virtually identical. Given that blacks and Hispanics are more likely to live in neighborhoods with lower real estate values, these groups are actually less exposed than they might be.

So the charge of racism cannot be made *even on the empirical evidence.* Nonwhites simply are not more likely to live near toxic waste sites than whites.

Nevertheless, "environmental racism" is viewed as such a daunting, intractable form of discrimination that a National People of Color Leadership Summit on the Environment was held in Washington, D.C. to devise solutions to the problem. Other minority environmental groups have been formed for the sole purpose of combatting this scourge.

There is even a graduate course taught at Yale on the subject. Entitled, "Environmental Justice: Issues of Racism, Poverty and the Environment," the program "examines distinct responses to racism and poverty in the form of movements for social and economic justice" and focuses "on the activities of a traditional, white-dominated environmental movement."

An interesting case of "environmental racism" occurred in Louisiana in 1997, when Shintech, a Japanese corporation, proposed building a polyvinyl chloride plastics plant in St. James Parish, which is about half black. Southern University Professor Florence Robinson stated that Shintech targeted St. James because blacks are confined to "certain neighborhoods." Joining local activists, she asserted that an environmental injustice was taking place "for the alleged good of society" and that such plants were never placed in affluent, white neighborhoods, as if it were a matter of race, not economics.

Due to local pressure, the EPA ordered a review of the air quality permits given to Shintech, in order to allow for more time to investigate environmental injustice. Shockingly, the state's NAACP President, Ernest Johnson, announced his neutrality on the Shintech plant, stating that he resented the manner in which plant opponents were raising unfounded claims of racism. Prof. Robinson replied that Johnson's NAACP "is not the NAACP of Thurgood Marshall... and people who put their lives on the line."

In other words, Johnson was fair and reasonable enough to examine the facts and avoid the temptation to claim bigotry when everyone else around him was grasping for the last refuge of scoundrels.

HIV: A Very Strange "Civil Right"

The predictions nine years ago that the Americans with Disabilities Act (ADA) would prove to be a monstrous and unreasonable burden for private industry and even government have by and large come true. Presented as a "civil rights" bill which would prohibit discrimination against people in wheelchairs and others afflicted with conditions generally thought of as "handicapping," was vaguely worded and ridiculously open-ended.

The result has not only been the costly and useless creation of wheelchair ramps that are never utilized, but claims of "discrimination" that defy common sense and anything reasonable Americans would consider to be a legitimate strike against unfairness. Indeed, there have been some outlandish lawsuits filed in the name of the "disabled." As it turns out, any perversion or peculiarity might be included in the definition of "handicapped."

In September of 1994, Sidney Abbot went to the office of Dr. Randon Bragdon, a dentist in Bangor, Maine, complaining of a toothache. When she informed Dr. Bragdon that she was HIV positive, he did not refuse to treat her. What he did tell her was that he would have to treat her at a local hospital because his office lacked the proper facilities to protect himself and his assistants from possible infection. Since even the most minor dental treatment involves invasive procedures, Dr. Bragdon's position could only be described as reasonable to a fault. Given the fact that he is in private practice, he conceivably could have refused to treat her at all.

Nevertheless, Abbott's response, with assistance from radical homosexual organizations, was to file a civil rights lawsuit against Dr. Bragdon under the federal Americans with Disabilities Act. Abbott claims that being infected with HIV entitles her to protection under ADA and that treating her any differently from other patients violates her civil rights.

Abbott's lawyers, led by Bennett Klein of the Boston-based

Gay & Lesbian Advocates and Defenders, claim that for Abbott to travel 45 minutes to a local hospital and pay an extra $185 is discrimination.

Abbott admitted in her own sworn testimony in her deposition that the case was a set-up against Dr. Bragdon. Back in 1991, soon after the ADA was passed, a complaint was filed against him by Douglas Worster-Jones, who had full blown AIDS and whom Dr. Bragdon told he would have to treat in a local hospital. The complaint continued even after Worster-Jones' death, when his estate sued Dr. Bragdon for $5,000. The case was eventually dropped.

But the radicals were not through with Dr. Bragdon. He points out that doctors and dentists follow universal precautions, which in his case, cost him $45,000 annually in office preparation against people who lie about the diseases they have or do not know. He does state that most people with HIV will admit it and are willing to go to the hospital for the best care and so as to not put other people at risk.

But the insanity of radical homosexuals knows no bounds as they pursue a perverted "civil rights" cause. Abbott, who was traveling Maine lecturing about AIDS, was directed to Dr. Bragdon's office by Sally Lou Patterson, the director of the Eastern Maine AIDS Network. Abbott admitted that Patterson had informed her of the Worster-Jones case and the opportunity to sue Dr. Bragdon. She said in her deposition, "I understood that if Dr. Bragdon would not treat me, I would be taking legal action against him." She also conceded that she was not actually impaired by her HIV status.

Dr. Bragdon has likely been targeted because he has advocated the establishment of hospital-based dental clinics to treat HIV-positive patients, a concept that is anathema to AIDS activist radicals. He says, "I'm not going to forget my training because some people have gone crazy with the politics of this." He says that when doctors become aware that a patient is HIV positive and someone gets a needle stick from a needle that had been used on the patient, they are supposed to go on the anti-HIV drug AZT and other anti-viral drugs within one to two hours and avoid sexual contact for six to nine months. Hardly a small risk.

"I don't believe they have a right to tell me or anyone else that

I have to take these risks," Dr. Bragdon says.

So what started as yet another fanatical liberal attempt to govern with emotion rather than common sense has grown into another law out of control. The "civil rights" madness that has dominated political discourse in America has taken yet one more turn into the realm of lunacy.

"Americans" With Foreign Loyalties

Richard Pastorella did not see the Puerto Rican FALN terrorists celebrating their freedom on television, although he knows everything about it. He did not see them waving the Puerto Rican flag amidst cheers in Puerto Rico and Chicago, although those scenes made him sick to stomach. Pastorella, in fact, cannot see at all.

Blinded by the exploding bombs planted by FALN terrorists who conspired with those just released, Pastorella has not seen anything for seventeen years. Pastorella, along with his fellow New York City police detectives Rocco Pascarella and Anthony Senft — who also suffered permanent crippling injuries because of FALN terrorism — has been making the rounds of talk shows, protesting the gross injustice of Bill Clinton's clemency to people who conspired to cause similar injuries to roughly 130 people.

In the name of independence for Puerto Rico, FALN sympathizers and a small cadre of America-hating thugs in the United States Congress, believe that terrorists who use bombs instead of ballots on American soil ought to be granted clemency for their crimes. This says as much about Representatives Jose Serrano and Nydia Velazquez as it does about hoodlums Edwin Cortes and Dylcia Pagan, both of whom owe their lives to a United States Senate run by Hillary Clinton.

While the political motivations of the President are clear to anyone who has even remotely followed his actions for seven years, it is an established fact that the strategy backfired badly. In his biggest miscalculation since the failed health care takeover, Clinton pardoned eleven terrorists in one day, after pardoning only three other people in six and a half years. Although the move was nakedly political, it raises some interesting points which are so obvious they are actually ignored.

What has been lost in all this is exactly why the Clintons believed such a policy would help Hillary with Puerto Rican voters. Certainly, it is unclear as to precisely what percentage of Puerto Rican voters support independence. Only four percent of Puerto Ricans on the island voted for independence in last year's plebiscite (the rest splitting between statehood and remaining a commonwealth.) But the independence issue is beside the point.

Then there is the terrorism issue. There may be Puerto Rican voters (Americans) who support independence, yet do not favor the use of violence to achieve that end. There have already been supporters of the clemency who have come forward and maintained that they, in fact, support statehood. So the actual points of view on the status of the island seem to have no difference on clemency or support for the FALN. Ultimately, however, all of this is also beside the point.

What *is* the issue is the fact that the Clinton pardon (assuming it was politically motivated to assist Hillary) is an admission that race and ethnicity are destiny in American politics. Consider: Hillary Clinton, an *American* politician and wife of the President of the United States, is running for a seat in the *United States* Senate. This is an *American* election in which only *Americans* can vote. So even the most brazenly transparent political maneuver still must necessarily be aimed at appealing to *American* voters.

Yet, what have the Clintons done? They have enacted a policy which is perceived to be in the interests of a foreign nation, in the hopes that the "American" voters they have targeted will vote based on caring about this foreign nation (Puerto Rico) more than they care about the United States.

It is disingenuous, to say the least, to argue that Puerto Rico is not a foreign nation and is, in fact, a part of the United States. This is only true in a literal legal sense. Culturally, Puerto Rico is obviously a distinct and separate nation. Even those Puerto Ricans who favor statehood or commonwealth status do so, according to surveys, for purely economic reasons. Puerto Rico fields its own Olympic team and its fans cheer loudest when they play the United States.

In any other country in the world, it goes without saying that, whatever other differences citizens may have, they certainly agree on wanting what is best for their country. Only in America do politicians pander to "Americans" whose loyalties are to foreign nations.

Was Jesus Homeless?

During the Democratic National Convention in the summer of 1992, Jesse Jackson, in a roaring prime time speech, referred to the baby Jesus as "homeless." This came as shocking news to theologians and Bible students, as well as mainstream Christians, and other ecclesiastical historians. It also would have been quite a surprise to Joseph and Mary, not to mention Saints Luke and Matthew, among others.

In making his political point against heartless Republicans, Jackson singlehandedly rewrote the story of the most famous birth of all time. That same week, the indefatigable Ray Kerrison of the *New York Post*, wrote that upon hearing Jackson's words, he "nearly fell off my chair." In fact, Kerrison was so thrown by Jackson's statement (remember, Jackson is an ordained Christian minister) that he actually took the time to consult several noted theologians before writing his column. They confirmed, naturally, that the good Reverend was, as usual, on another planet.

Ignorance on the birth of Jesus is inexcusable for anyone who is even remotely familiar with this sacred chapter of history. But for a man of the cloth, it is incomprehensible—unless one assumes that

Jackson's revisionism was deliberate — intended to underscore an ideological imperative. This probably was the case, which then calls into question the character of someone who would rewrite the Bible for his own political ends.

Now New York City Mayor Rudy Giuliani has put forth a "homeless" policy—requiring the able-bodied to work if they want to avail themselves of city shelters—which has left-wing dinosaurs cackling about his heartlessness during this holy time of year, bemoaning the self-created plight of bums and winos, and yes, once again invoking the name of Jesus. Merry Christmas to you, too.

This time it is the First Lady of Chappaqua, New York — Giuliani's opponent for the United States Senate — who has the Gospel authors turning in their graves. Hillary Clinton, whose version of the Scriptures does not exactly measure up to the Acts of the Apostles, has profoundly proclaimed that the Christmas season is a celebration of "the birth of a homeless child." (Now New Yorkers know that the Wild Man of 96th Street is 2000 years old.) Al Gore has also referred to Jesus as "homeless."

In fact, the most detailed account of the birth of Jesus is found in the Gospel according to Luke. It is also found in Matthew's Gospel. Luke, whose Gospel is "dominated by historical perspective," according to the Confraternity of Christian Doctrine, authored his work in large part by consulting actual witnesses. In the case of the Christmas story, his source was Jesus's mother, Mary, whose credibility would probably be regarded as impeccable, even by Hillary and Jesse Jackson.

According to Luke, in order to comply with an order from Caesar Augustus that all persons return to their places of birth so as to be registered for taxation purposes, Joseph took Mary from his home in Nazareth and departed for Bethlehem. The Gospel says, "It came to pass that there went out a decree from Caesar Augustus that all the world should be taxed." The emperor demanded that "all the inhabited world be registered." This was the process of a census, an expedient method of taxation.

As a Jew, Joseph was required to go "into Judea, unto the city of David, which is called Bethlehem" since he was "of the house and lineage of David." With so many returning people in Bethlehem for registration, there were very few vacancies, thus the shortage of temporary places of shelter. Mary was about to give birth to "her first child, a son" and "as there was no place for them inside the inn, she wrapped him up and laid him in a manger." And, as the saying goes, the rest is history.

Soon after, the Holy Family returned home to Nazareth. Jesus, therefore, was never "homeless" in any sense of the word, whether by the standards of His own time or in today's jargon. So Hillary Clinton, always the first to wail about the injection of religion into politics, saw fit to affect current social policy by pointing to the Nativity to support her views.

Although Hillary claims to have spoken recently to Eleanor Roosevelt on a number of issues, it is unclear as to whether she consulted her on this particular pressing problem. Moreover, Hillary, according to most notable theologians, is not mentioned anywhere in the Bible. However, on the matter of all the trouble people were made to endure so that "all the world should be taxed," Caesar Augusta would certainly find Hillary to be an enthusiastic proponent of his wealth redistribution scheme.

White Sports Mascots an American Tradition

The explosion of multicultural madness in the 1990's, coupled with political correctness as the new and bizarre orthodoxy on the American scene, has buttressed racial paranoia to the point of hysteria. Calls to conform all aspects of American culture to the brave new world of thought control have manifested themselves in some of the most insane causes imaginable. One of the chic demands made by the PC police has been leveled at sports franchises to change the names of their teams and mascots, which offend the sensibilities of radical Indian activists.

As a result, the famed basketball team of St. John's University changed its name from the Redmen in 1994 to the Red Storm. Another Big East basketball team, Syracuse, changed its name 20 years earlier from the Indians to the Orangemen, after the fruit, of all things. But this doesn't appear to be an issue that is dying.

Suzan Shown Harjo is probably the leading "Native American" activist dedicated to the wasteful endeavor of cracking down on Indian sports names. The most offensive name, in her view, is "Redskin," the moniker of Washington's storied NFL franchise. She refers to the term as the "r-word." According to Harjo, more than 1,000 sports teams in America -- representing schools at all levels -- have cast aside their Indian names since 1970. But she's hardly through with her crusade. The major professional sports franchises are the fish she still wants to fry.

Last week, Harjo appeared on Fox network debating the issue with constitutional attorney Ann Coulter. Harjo spouted the usual bromides that Indian names were "offensive," demeaning and cast "Native Americans" as somehow subhuman. Other ethnic groups, she maintained, are not made into mascots. Coulter countered that in a national poll, a majority of Indians supported the concept of using Indian names for sports teams, as a matter of honor and prestige. While Harjo disputed the poll findings, she remarked to Coulter, a leggy, attractive blonde, "How would you like it if they called a sports team, 'The Blondes'"? Coulter, not missing a beat, replied, "That would be so cool!"

So what are the facts on sports teams and their names and mascots? In the four major sports -- football, baseball, basketball and hockey -- which total 131 teams in all -- there are six teams which go by Indian names. They are the Chicago Black Hawks (hockey), the Golden State Warriors (basketball), Cleveland Indians and Atlanta Braves (baseball), and the Kansas City Chiefs and Washington Redskins (football).

In what is undoubtedly startling news to the new Thought Police and racial avengers, there are as many as *23 teams* which bear names symbolizing Caucasians, Europeans and their descendants. While not all are explicitly racial or ethnic, even those signifying certain occupations are unquestionably pertaining to white people. (And these 23 teams do not count the "Fighting Irish" of Notre Dame, a college football team.)

The Vancouver Canucks and Montreal Canadiens (hockey) are both representative of French Canadians. The Boston Celtics (basketball) clearly represent a historic people of Europe, more specifically of the United Kingdom. The Minnesota Vikings (football) represent the Nordic or Scandinavian peoples, and the Viking mascot is a white man with a big beard and sword. Vikings were often seen as raiders or invaders of sorts, so the team not only represents a white group, but a group often engaged in international criminality. In the case of the Pittsburgh Pirates (baseball) and Tampa Bay Buccaneers (football), whites are overtly represented as criminals, yet everyone accepts this all in good fun, looking instead at the masculine and rugged qualities of these groups, which is why teams were named after them in the first place. The Oakland Raiders (football) fall into the same category, with a Caucasian marauder as the team's symbol. The team has always been known for its physical style of play and its silver and black uniform colors.

Other famous teams also overtly represent Caucasian peoples. The New York Knickerbockers (basketball) received their moniker in tribute to Dutch settlers of New York State. While Cowboys could technically be of any race, the Dallas football team was clearly modeled on the traditional white cowpoke. The New England Patriots (football) were based on the white American patriots of Boston, and even the fabled New York Yankees derived their name from northern Caucasians, more specifically white Union soldiers, with the term "Yankee" usually one of derision.

Less overtly racial but still based on white men are the New York Rangers (hockey), Texas Rangers (baseball), Ottawa Senators (hockey), Los Angeles Kings (hockey), Sacramento Kings (basketball), Cleveland Cavaliers (basketball), Kansas City Royals (baseball), Seattle Mariners (baseball), San Francisco 49ers (football), Pittsburgh Steelers (football), and even the beloved New York Mets -- short for Metropolitans, signifying white New Yorkers of a different era.

While the multicultural fanatics are on a roll, why not consider teams that may be construed to be making a mockery of religion, specifically Catholics? The New Orleans Saints (football), Anaheim Angels (baseball), San Diego Padres (baseball), and New Jersey Devils (hockey) all fit this particular bill.

Ironically, sitting on the sidelines throughout this debate are the blacks, who finally have a legitimate gripe: they are *not represented* by any American sports teams, despite comprising most of the players!

What to Do About "The Sopranos"

Amidst all the hysteria surrounding "The Sopranos" and the popular show's alleged anti-Italian bias, a calm, rational assessment of all the facts -- tangible, social and political -- are necessarily required in order for fair-minded people to make a judgement before this entire episode spirals into complete madness.

It is quite true that there is a double standard (or, in fact, several different standards) when it comes to the portrayal of ethnic and racial groups in popular culture. These differing portrayals have nothing whatsoever to do with the actual reality of life in America, and everything to do with political correctness and the disinclination to offend radical ethnic and racial interest groups. For example, on television and in the movies, blacks are invariably portrayed to an inordinate extent as computer geniuses, heroic doctors and generally benevolent, moral and sober. There are, of course, some blacks who fit these descriptions. But if Hollywood were to be concerned with a totally accurate reflection of reality, most street criminals would be black and most heroic doctors and computer geniuses white.

This is not to say that Hollywood ought to be bound by reality, but these facts must be taken into account when the racial sirens start complaining. And even with this consistently unrealistic favorable portrayal, blacks radicals *still* complain about their screen images.

Now, it is also quite true that some groups are treated in a slipshod manner by comparison. Anti-Christian and anti-Catholic bias are definitely prevalent, especially if one defines "bias" as treatment that would not be given to another group. The recent uproars attached to blasphemous works of "art" depicting unflattering and outrageous images of Jesus and the Blessed Mother arose not only because of the extreme nature of the paintings, but even more so because Catholics know damn well that such disrespect would never have been levelled at black or Jewish icons. Anti-Christian bias is indeed, as one writer put it, "the last proper bigotry." The Martin Scorsese film, "The Last Temptation of Christ," which was a depiction of Jesus as having succumbed to sexual temptation, was certainly an affront to Catholic sensibilities.

But unlike the artwork (which was underwritten with tax dollars) and, to a lesser extent, "The Last Temptation of Christ," which insulted a particular icon, "The Sopranos" simply does not fall into the same category. So-called "Italian spokesmen" (whatever that is) complain that "The Sopranos" portrays Italians as brutal criminals with vulgar mouths; as simpletons and, most offensively, as mobsters -- playing right into the stereotype.

In fact, what the show does is portray *these particular fictitious Italians* that way, not Italians in general. What are the producers to do? For goodness sake, you couldn't get a good mob show off the ground if you tried to portray them as a simply swell bunch. The fact that the players are Italian-Americans is simply rooted in fact. Historically in America (although it is now changing) most mobsters have been Italians, even though most Italians have not been mobsters. FBI crime figures have been stubbornly consistent in this regard -- less than one-tenth of one percent of Italian-Americans have been associated with organized crime. The new Italian crusaders should point this out if it makes them feel better, and as often as possible if it serves as a kind of therapy for them.

What has become clear is that the self-appointed Italian spokesmen are not in step with Italians in general, who view themselves primarily as Americans, and who generally enjoy "The Sopranos" because it is a finely acted, entertaining piece of fiction.

What is also becoming clear is that Italian sirens risk coming off like the radical blacks and Hispanics, who spend most of their lives with massive chips on their shoulders, searching for, flailing at, and whining about every perceived slight.

Plainly, Italian-Americans are among the most conservative groups in the United States. Undoubtedly, they privately scoff at the blacks for their constant complaining. That Italians are above this is a sign of their confidence in themselves and in their place in America. The new Italian sirens reek of a very embarrassing paranoia that borders on hysterics.

Italian-Americans would do well to address genuine problems that affect them, like anti-white affirmative action, set asides and quotas, all of which keep Italians from jobs and positions they deserve. Third world immigration is killing white neighborhoods. Moreover, Italians face the same obstacles that all whites encounter in America -- a leftist media double standard that highlights white crime and downplays non-white brutality. These, of course, are the issues that genuinely hurt Italians. But some politicians simply have too much time on their hands, or are too preoccupied with what appears on cable television to address them.

Sensitivity is out of control in America. Italian-Americans, more properly known as Americans, should stay clear of petty nonsense and leave racial and ethnic paranoia to Al Sharpton and Abe Foxman. Sit back and enjoy the show.

The Source

What was originally known as "rap" music, but is now more commonly referred to as "hip-hop," is not merely a *type* of music, but can more accurately be characterized as a "culture" or a way of being, much as rock music in the late 1960's was associated with hippies, drugs and Woodstock. While "hip-hop" has never become as mainstream as rock 'n roll, it nevertheless has a highly discernible fan base and a huge following.

Although hip-hop does not explicitly identify itself as exclusively black, and is not in all instances anti-white, the racial consciousness of rap is clearly informed by its blackness. Hip-hop is an enormous industry with a handful of publications dedicated to it. The largest and most notable of these is *The Source*, a slick monthly magazine which identifies itself as "The magazine of hip-hop music, culture and politics." A single issue is close to 300 pages for the newsstand price of $2.95, but the truly fanatical can subscribe for $12.95 per year.

What exists inside *The Source* is a culture so alien to the American mainstream as to be virtually unintelligible. What began in 1988 as a one-page newsletter is now the bible of what can be thought of as "hip-hop nation." Its pages are filled with articles about rap performers and their music. While any directory of periodicals would list *The Source* as published in English, the fact is that virtually all of the interviews are in Ebonics (black English), making the words incomprehensible to the average person. Almost all rappers go by names like Puff Daddy, Da Brat, Snoop Dog and Ghostface Killah. The Ebonics is often words deliberately misspelled so that they read the way they are said ("niggas", "boyz", "gangstas", "hoes', etc.) Newly created, non-grammatical words like "theyself" also grace its pages.

A typical exchange printed in *The Source* requires a translator. From an interview with rapper Lil Wayne:

The Source: "Whut is a Hot Boy?"

Lil Wayne: "A paper chaser who got his block on fire. Remain in the G until the moment he expires. Know what it is to make somethin' out of nuthin.' Handle his biz and don't be cryin' and sufferin'."

While this excerpt is unreadable it is actually quite benign. Most exchanges in *The Source* reek with profanity and obscenity. From the same interview with Lil Wayne:

The Source: "Whut color is the inside of a whale?"

Lil Wayne: "The inside of a whale... I don't fuckin' know. But the inside of a pussy is pink."

The Source: Whut's the first thing you do when a girl backs that ass up?"

Lil Wayne: "Make her drop it like it's hot."

The Source: "Whut's the first thing you do after a show?"

Lil Wayne: "Fuck a ho, slang dick."

Although *The Source* is mostly geared to men, female rapper Da Brat was no less articulate. Asked how she was going to promote her next album, she responded, "The album cover is going to be tight, wet and squeezing... Hopefully niggas will say, 'damn, I wanna fuck her,' so I can get the record sales goin'."

Rap lyrics themselves frequently urge the murder of whites ("devils"), particularly police. One urged the slaying of Mayor Giuliani. From the song "Sweatin Bullets," by Brand Nubian: "These devils make me sick. I love to fill them full of holes; kill them all in the daytime, broad mother fucking daylight; 12 o'clock, grab the Glock; why wait for night?"

The Source reviewed an album by the group Hypnotize Camp, which included songs titled, "Project Hoes" and "Dick Suckin' Hoes."

So popular is *The Source* among blacks that half its pages are advertisements from giants such as Foot Locker, Nike, Nintendo, Calvin Klein and Tommy Hilfiger. No "diversity is our strength" nonsense in *The Source*. All of the faces in the ads are of black people. Photos in the magazine of black men are practically interchangeable. Almost all have angry, glaring looks on their faces. Hip-hop dress features gold chains, bracelets and rings, kerchiefs on the head, as well as pants hanging so low that the underwear shows.

Many of the men are also bare-chested and have tattoos. All of this presumably is keeping with the "gangsta" image. In *The Source*, the word "Blacks" is always spelled with a capital "B" while "whites" always appears in the small case.

The Source also has political articles, all of which advance the black cause. In an interview with San Francisco Mayor Willie Brown, *The Source* refers to California initiatives intended to dismantle affirmative action. Brown refers disdainfully to "the old conservative white guys" who feel their power slipping away.

In a section called Media Watch, the magazine monitors national media coverage of hip-hop. Quoting a Puerto Rican in the New York *Daily News* who was upset over Puerto Rican singer Jennifer Lopez's association with black rapper Sean "Puffy" Combs (who had been arrested on a gun charge), *The Source* responded, "If Puffy were white, we doubt the media would make it a point to print random quotes from people who think Jennifer should dump Puff."

In its publisher's credo, *The Source* bills itself as a "voice for the Hip-Hop Nation." It is entirely appropriate that the word "nation" is used, as *The Source* is not only non-conformist but alien to the core.

AIDS: The Great White Plot

It is not enough that radical homosexuals blame the AIDS epidemic on Republicans and conservatives, rather than on their own disgusting and outrageous behavior. The homosexual party line is that by "cutting" funding for AIDS research (which, incidentally, is higher than for all other diseases), government officials are somehow responsible for the spread of this scourge. Homosexuals have also sought to blame the lack of "sex education" in schools for the epidemic. In fact, this peculiar movement, which identifies itself by its perversions, has succeeded in attaching blame for AIDS on everyone imaginable, with one exception — themselves — which is clearly where the fault entirely belongs. One Reagan Administration official remarked before his death from AIDS, "The disease could be stopped tomorrow if gays would just stop fucking each other in the ass."

There is a new scapegoat on the horizon, however. In some ways it is an old story, and the perpetrator has already been blamed for most of the ills afflicting mankind throughout history. Now, the AIDS epidemic is yet another evil which can be attributed to the sinister workings of... the white race.

New African, a glossy magazine with a circulation of 32,000 in 40 countries, is one of Africa's most respected publications. It is published by Baffour Ankomah, a London-based Ghanaian, and its articles are reprinted in different publications across Africa. So influential is *New African*, that its editorials are picked up worldwide.

In a recent diatribe, Ankomah wrote, "...what we call AIDS is actually U.S. biological warfare gone wrong." So there it is. A widely read international journal promoting the nonsensical theory that whites are deliberately orchestrating a grand plan to infect blacks around the world and Africans in particular. Ankomah continues, "Africa is the target of the world AIDS cartel. They want to pin it on us, to destroy us with it."

According to *New African*, AIDS is a money-making hoax perpetrated by the United Nations and the whites who control it. (It's news, by the way, that whites control the U.N.) Ankomah denies the reported AIDS death tolls for Africa and claims that if Africans are dying of AIDS it can only be due to a Western plot to rid the world of Africans.

New African is currently urging its readers to ignore all health warnings about AIDS and not to use condoms. No point in following the instructions of those who are in on the plot. Medical workers in Africa are dumbfounded at how much influence the magazine is having on citizens and are bemoaning the fact that *New African*'s articles are creating a major obstacle for controlling the disease. Last year, Africa accounted for 83 percent of the entire world's

AIDS deaths.

Why do Africans and other blacks believe such nonsense? Lisa Jacobs, a spokeswoman for the U.N. AIDS program in Geneva is so duped by African sensitivities to patent foolishness that she is careful to temper her criticism. "It's important we don't just dismiss these theories as rantings in Africa," she says, "because many of the problems they point out have valid roots."

A more sensible reaction came from El Hadj Sy, a Senegalese United Nations AIDS worker, who tried to explain the bizarre popularity of Ankomah's theories. "People are desperate to find something to blame rather than their own behavior. They want to believe that something this evil must be inflicted upon our continent by outsiders."

Still, a more likely explanation is the very nature of Africans themselves, who tend to believe some of the most far-fetched and ridiculous ideas ever hatched by modern human beings. Stories abound about foreign correspondents who stagger back to civilization with tales of outlandish African beliefs: sorcerers who can steal a man's genitals with a handshake; religious fanatics who believe they can walk on water — and then drown; witches who call down lightning from the sky and who then must be burned to death. In short, Africans are ripe for credulity and other forms of superstition. The white AIDS plot is actually a mild belief by comparison.

In Alameda County, California, blacks are five times more likely to get AIDS than whites, yet blacks are so notoriously resistant to warnings about AIDS, that shock billboards have been placed in areas where black homosexuals are known to frequent. The billboards, which show one naked black man lying on top of another, state, "Been there. Done that. Get HIV tested. It could save your life."

But even in America, surveys show that fully one-third of blacks either outright believe or believe possible the notion that AIDS was created by white scientists in order to be used as a genocidal tool against blacks. Clearly, this shows a profound degree of gullibility among blacks, coupled with the widespread belief that whites are so implacably racist that blacks will accept just about any fantastic piece of nonsense that buttresses their notion of white wickedness.

Dr. Laura and the New Censorship

Radical homosexuals and other putrid leftists have amply demonstrated their hypocrisy and tyrannical leanings in their war with radio host Laura Schlessinger, who now plans her new television show for the fall. What drives them crazy is that Dr. Laura has so many listeners. If she was unsuccessful, they could allow her to fade away in her own poor ratings. But Schlessinger is so revered that the long arm of brute force is the only way they can stop giving the American people what they want. When the free market doesn't satisfy their degenerate demands, they simply hold a gun to the head of the television executives. It won't work.

And exactly what has Dr. Laura said that has the homosexuals soaking themselves in lavender? "If you're gay or lesbian, it's a biological error that inhibits you from relating normally to the opposite sex. The fact that you are intelligent, creative and valuable is all true. The error is in your ability to relate sexually intimately, in a loving way to a member of the opposite sex. It is a biological error: Nobody said they were 'bad people' or incompetent or not intelligent or not good citizens. They just said the sexual behavior is deviant and we don't want it in schools, and we don't want it to be recognized on the same level as heterosexuality."

Schlessinger, a devoutly religious Jew, also has thoughts on same-sex parenting. "It's not normal. It's not in the best interest of children. This is a travesty that these two lesbians were given two little children, intentionally depriving them of a father: It's despicable. It's unhealthy. "On "gay rights" she says "Rights. Rights? For sexual deviants... there are now rights. That's what I'm worried about, with all the pedophilia and the bestiality and the sadomasochism and the cross-dressing. Is this all going to be 'rights,' too, to deviant sexual behavior? Why does deviant sexual behavior get rights? "And, "When we have the word 'homosexual,' we are clarifying the dysfunction, the deviancy, the reality. We change it to 'gay' and it makes it more difficult to pinpoint the truth. So one of the things the homosexual agenda did was to change the name. Well, 'homosexuality' is the truth. 'Gay' isn't."

In the world of broadcasting, it is purely natural that a radio host who attracts 15-20 million listeners a week because of these sensible views be given a television show. Networks are in the business to make money and they clearly see a gold mine with Dr. Laura. Moreover, Dr. Laura has a following that money can't buy. It would be unnatural to deny her a show because a handful of freaks are upset about it.

So not only do the homosexuals say to hell with the free market and the legitimate appetite of viewers -- there is a supposed "higher standard" to uphold -- they ignore the abject failures of their own agenda. Ellen DeGeneres is a genuinely funny comic, both as a stand-up and in her acting. (Ellen has since done a swell sex scene with Sharon Stone -- lucky stiff!)

By all accounts, her rise to stardom was the result of her talent and audience affection for her. She was fighting no cause and stood for no political agenda. It was only *after* she came out as a lesbian, after it became the focal point of her show, and after she became the poster child for organized gaydom did her show's ratings plummet. The American viewers did not care much for a comedy that revolved around a lesbian plot, purely for the sake of it.

In the instance of "Ellen," the radicals took the opposite tack. They insisted ABC not cancel the show, *despite* poor ratings. But these activists are in reality unprincipled and hypocritical, and in ways beyond disdaining the free market. Christine Quinn, for example, a New York City lesbian councilwoman, is one of the chief fire breathers trying to thwart the beginning of Dr. Laura's show.

She is a ringleader for the cause simply because she does not like Schlessinger's views. The American viewer doesn't count, nor does the concept of free speech and expression. The new censors are just the old totalitarians.

But lesbian Quinn is ultimately transparent in her advocacy -- imparting a double standard that she only half-heartedly tries to hide. Last year, when the controversy over the sacrilege "art" at the Brooklyn Museum broke out regarding a painting of the Blessed Mother doused with elephant dung, Quinn defended it. She still does. She claims that to inhibit the showing of the painting in any way amounts to censorship. The huge difference between Dr. Laura's show and the museum painting -- in addition to Dr. Laura having the support of the public and being the result of supply and demand -- is that the painting was partly funded with tax dollars. Clearly this makes the case against the painting more intellectually justifiable -- never to ban it, but simply to have the free market decide and not force taxpayers to underwrite it.

Incredibly, not only does lesbian Quinn profess to not see it that way, she actually argues the opposite point. When pressed by reporters and other interviewers as to how she can consistently, as a matter of claimed principle, defend the heretical painting's right to public display, decrying censorship, while at the same time advocating the ban of a television show she wants deep-sixed because of an ideological difference, she also mentions the taxpayer funding angle. She says *because* it is taxpayer financed it should be displayed! In other words, it is legitimate to ban free speech and expression when no one is forced to pay for it and when the public demands that speech and expression. But it is also legitimate to force Americans to pay for something which they would never otherwise agree to pay for and display it against the will of a free market.

Even Quinn herself appears somewhat uncomfortable making this argument with a straight face, but the new censors are not bound by any sort of coherent logic. They want what they want, period. Intellectual justification and principle can be awkwardly concocted after the fact. In the end, the new censorship will fail and Dr. Laura will continue to speak the truth to the majority of Americans who like her and agree with her.

The Problem With Islam

The religion of Islam is alien to virtually all Americans. Only a minuscule number of people in the United States can actually claim to truly understand it, and those are essentially limited to Moslems themselves. Non-Moslems who grasp Islam are undoubtedly within the realm of diplomats and professors of theology or experts in the Middle East. Although Islam is a worldwide religion, it has its roots and is practiced in its most unfiltered form in the lands of Arabia.

Because of the war on terrorism, American politicians have uttered some of the most uninformed bromides one could possibly hear on the subject of Islam. People who have never so much as touched a Koran are claiming to know what Islam does and does not stand for.

With President Bush and his minions so painstakingly iterating that this is "a war against terrorism, not Islam," and that hostility against Moslems in general is a sin, it has become thoroughly unfashionable to admit that many Americans are uncomfortable with a significant Moslem presence in America. While America boasts of its historical pluralism, that pluralism is, of course, largely a myth. America is indeed a "Christian" nation -- not solely in a theological sense, but absolutely in a cultural sense. That is why Jews have so successfully assimilated into America; the common cultural ancestors of both sets of beliefs are extraordinarily compatible.

Islam, on the other hand, is an entirely different matter. America's experience with Islam is limited, making it easy to examine. Even in the 21st Century, most of the world lives in the "not free" category, as defined by the Rand Institute. Virtually all of the world's democracies reside in polities peopled by Western Christians. The notions of separation of church and state, equality of the sexes, freedom of speech and press, and religious pluralism are unheard of in most of the Moslem world. Ordinary Americans can see this. It is not merely a perception; it is a fact.

Certainly, it would be unfair to label Islam a religion of terrorism. Murder and atrocities have been committed by fanatics of many religions and ideologies. Crimes have been perpetrated in the names of Christianity, atheism (Communism), nationalism, Judaism and the desire for ethnic or tribal autonomy. But -- and here's the clincher -- there is no discernible Christian minority in the United States that would support the deliberate slaughter of 5,000 innocent civilians for any cause, even one they deemed worthwhile. There is clearly such a segment in the Moslem world, even within American borders.

It is impossible to quantify an exact number, but average Americans know full well that there is a portion of the Moslem population in America that celebrated with great joy the mass murder of September 11. The celebrations were highly visible in Moslem countries around the world. So what is it, Americans wonder, that makes harboring such feelings compatible with the religion of Islam?

On the same note, American politicians, famous for their feckless pandering to voters and interest groups, are never said to have to worry about a group of organized Christians who support, say, Timothy McVeigh. Murderous extremists are denounced and dismissed in America and they control no voting segment whatsoever because such a discernible segment is non-existent. In the Moslem world, conversely, not a day goes by when diplomats or Middle East experts are not bemoaning the fact that America's Moslem friends and coalition partners are subject to domestic politics -- that they must pay lip service to the segments of their populations which harbor virulently anti-American feelings and espouse support and outright happiness at the slaughter of Americans.

Moreover, there is no Western country where it is illegal to convert to Islam or practice it. There are mosques rising at record pace in America and across Europe. Yet in Algeria and other Moslem polities, Christianity is either outlawed or its practitioners are an oppressed minority. The idea that one of America's demands at the conclusion of the war will be greater openness to Christianity in Moslem countries is a pipe dream. It is akin to stuffing a square peg into a round hole. Cultures that are historically intolerant and undemocratic will not suddenly become enlightened bastions of libertarianism.

All of this gives rise to the obvious question of whether Islam is compatible at all with Western liberty and democracy. America's first internal experience with Islam was with the black Muslims, a group that is almost always peaceful and law-abiding, but which distinguished itself through its alienness to the United States. Muhammad Ali refused induction into the army because of his prime loyalty to his religion. The Nation of Islam itself is defined by its being a separate "nation." Of course, there are nuances and different interpretations to all religions. Many Moslems have fought bravely on the side of America and some Christians have refused to fight as conscientious objectors. But it is the preponderance of activities that matter, not merely isolated anecdotes. Although Catholicism, as a religion, is an undemocratic monarchy, it does not impose itself on the free democratic choices of individual Catholics living in free societies.

September 11 has changed the way America conducts itself in countless ways. Secretary of State Colin Powell, in a talk unthinkable even six months ago, articulated bravely and intelligently the need for the profiling of Arab and Moslem men. President Bush and Mayor Giuliani can attend interfaith services til kingdom come and it would not alter the intrinsic, unbridgeable chasm that exists between Islam and the West.

The Assault on Fishing

The problem with the "animal rights" crowd is that they take their philosophy to such a hysterical extreme that they fail in what would otherwise be a sensible goal. Anti-hunting, anti-fishing, pro-vegetarian groups cannot distinguish between arguments which even sportsmen find agreeable and the ridiculous demands that outfits like PETA (People for the Ethical Treatment of Animals) make.

There are two basic distinctions that the extremist groups are incapable of grasping. First, there is a difference between fishing, hunting and eating meat and the alleged cruelty that PETA swears is inherent in such actions. In fact, PETA asserts that one cannot engage in those things without also engaging in cruelty. This, of course, is patent nonsense. No self-respecting hunter or fisherman is interested in torturing animals and most do not. Sportsmen find mistreatment of animals abhorrent and conduct their sport humanely.

The second unbridgeable chasm between PETA and sensible people is strictly a matter of philosophy and values. PETA rejects the traditional and biblical axiom that God gave man dominion over the earth — that human beings were intended to hunt and harvest as a matter of survival. They deny that this is the natural order of things.

Moreover, and more shocking, is that groups like PETA see a complete moral equivalency between human beings and animals. The main tenet of "animal rights" is not merely that animals be treated humanely, but that they possess the exact same natural rights as people. They want this tenet codified in law. Therefore — and this is no exaggeration — they believe exterminating your home from termites is the same as killing a person. Plainly, this is in the realm of lunacy.

Currently, there is a bill in the House of Representatives (H.R. 3547, the Freedom to Fish Act) designed to protect fishing rights and ensure that federal regulations promote access for fishermen. The bill is largely in response to the outrageous attempts by PETA to have recreational fishing completely banned. PETA has even recruited a misguided 15 year old Boy Scout leader to take part in their anti-fishing ad campaigns.

Justin Aligata of Dallas is appearing in a television commercial urging other Boy Scouts not to fish, stating that fishing is in violation of Boy Scout law. According to PETA, "PETA has asked Boy Scouts of America President Milton H. Ward to withdraw the 'Fishing' and 'Fish and Wildlife Management' merit badges because they teach boys that hooking, suffocating, and killing fish is acceptable and to replace the badges with a 'Waterways Cleanup' badge."

In the commercial, young Justin says, "Boy Scout Law says we're not supposed to hurt or kill harmless things without reason. So I just couldn't hook helpless animals in the mouth, yank them out of their environment, and still call myself a Boy Scout."

PETA has some suggestions for young people in general. They include: "Put up signs at local fishing spots reading, 'Please do not leave fishing line here'... If someone asks you to go fishing, explain why you won't go. Tell them that fish have feelings and deserve to live just like anyone else. Suggest some of these activities instead: Frisbee, kite-flying, basketball, snorkeling, in-line skating, riding your bike, or bird watching. There are lots of ways to have fun outside without hurting your animal friends!"

PETA also suggests that children, "Create a 'fish-friendly' display for your local library. Include pictures of fish, useful facts, and information on why people shouldn't fish... Write a story from the perspective of a fish. Tell how things look from the fish's point of view. What things are important to the fish? What is he or she thinking?"

Some other gems include, "If your school fair has contests that give free goldfish as prizes, organize a group of students to complain to the principal. Explain that a frightened, lonely goldfish is no prize, and suggest stuffed animal toys or other non-animal prizes instead." And, "Don't buy tropical fish! Fish belong in open waters, and they are frustrated and unhappy when kept in tanks.

"If your town is holding a fishing tournament or other fishing event, hold a demonstration — it's easy, and it only takes a few people. Make some signs with slogans like 'Hooks Hurt' and 'Fishing Is No Fun for Fish' and stand outside the event. Pass out leaflets and tell people the fish's side of the story."

This assault on tradition and the American way of life is indeed the result of a backward value system — one Americans will certainly reject. And the assault on the Boy Scouts is the continuance of a disturbing trend aimed at undermining one of the last vestiges of bedrock American values.

Was Cleopatra Black?

One of the most insidious claims made by Afro-centrists is the fantasy that Cleopatra was black. In fact, many black "academics" have pronounced that all the major figures in ancient Egypt were of black African stock. While these proclamations comprise one of the major tenets of Afro-centrism, they are among the most easily disprovable. Among the other bizarre claims of Afro-centrists are that Moses and Jesus were also black. But what makes the Egyptian claim especially silly is the verifiable proof to the contrary.

When Afro-centric zealots decided to circulate the ridiculous notion about the race of the pharaohs, they probably failed to realize that their lies were so easily refuted by the existence of physiological and anthropometric evidence. Indeed, when concocting the fable that some ancient people were Negroid, the Egyptians were probably the worst choice. Quite inconveniently, the Egyptians left mummies.

It is an arduous endeavor, to say the least, to fabricate the race of a corpse which is so well-preserved that its eyelashes can be counted. Like their present-day counterparts, the ancient Egyptians were Caucasian, although with lighter skin. The DNA analysis of the pharaohs confirms this undeniably. Ramses II, who enslaved and persecuted the children of Israel, was probably a redhead. His corpse shows that he maintains the sharp features prominent in whites, as well as thin straight hair.

Although modern Egyptians are white, they are somewhat darker than the pyramid builders because of a higher intermarriage rate, largely permitted by the universalistic influence of Islam. The ancients were much more exclusionist.

After Afro-centrism reared its ugly head in the 1980's, John Leo, writing for *U.S. News & World Report*, contacted seven distinguished Egyptologists to obtain their views. All told Leo that neither the pharaohs nor Egypt's common people were Negroid. Predictably, none were willing to be quoted publicly, with one telling Leo the issue was "politically too hot." In the infancy of political correctness, even expert professors shied away from denouncing the most preposterous nonsense, as long as enough militant blacks were asserting it.

In addition to the existence of mummies, indications of the races of Old Testament figures are provided by the artists of ancient Egypt. Thousands of base relief carvings, wall paintings and decorative objects depicted a remarkably detailed record of the races of Egyptians and other peoples with which they had contact. The artists meticulously distinguished between races in all their works.

Greeks, Gergashites, Hittites, Amorites and Philistines were all drawn in minute detail. Racial differences in both facial features and skin color were pronounced. So careful were Egyptian artists in their detail, that their drawings were almost as much taxonomy as art.

A.A. Sayce and R. Peterson, in their book "Race in Ancient Egypt & the Old Testament," emphasized this point. They wrote, "The oldest surviving attempt to construct what we may call an ethnographic chart — that made in the tomb of the Theban prince Rekhm-Ra about a century before the birth of Moses — distinguishes between the Egyptians and their neighbors by portraying the black-skinned Negro, the olive-colored Syrians, the red-skinned Egyptian, and the white-skinned Libyan (then unmixed with the Arab hordes)..."

Like many peoples throughout history, Egyptians were often ruled by monarchs lighter-skinned than themselves. The queen Nefertiti was probably of Hittite stock, a group of European origin. In today's world, the group most representative of the ancient Egyptians are the Coptic Christians, who have been much more refrained from intermarriage.

Many of the early inhabitants of the Middle East may have had typically Northern European coloration. The Nile delta was originally settled by sandy-haired, blue-eyed people whose descendants continue to occupy most of present-day Morocco and Algeria. These ancients were probably descended from the Cro-Magnons, whose remains have been found in southern France. History records that these people — the first "Libyans" — were driven west of the Nile by the Egyptians. The artists depicted them with white skin. Amorites are shown to have had light hair and blue eyes.

King David was likely to have been fair-skinned, since the Israelites rarely intermarried. The giant Goliath, slain with a sling by David, was related to the Philistines, who were probably related to the Spartiate Greeks. Goliath's call for single combat was in following the Greek tradition.

Blacks, in contrast to all these groups, are depicted in ancient Egyptian art almost always as slaves or captives. The nonsense put forth by today's Afro-centrists is not so much an unworthy attempt at rewriting history, but a deliberate pack of lies designed to shred the truth of Western civilization.

Is Sex With Animals Normal?

If Peter Singer is not the most bizarre man in America, his pronouncements are unquestionably among the most peculiar, and even deranged, for a person who occupies a position of stature, prestige and influence. Considered the "father" of the modern "animal rights" movement, Singer invented the concept of "speciesism," which maintains that there is no moral distinction between human beings and non-human animals, and the killing of a rat is of no different consequence than the murder of a person.

Singer, appointed to an endowed chair in bioethics at Princeton University's Center for Human Values, is the author of the book *Practical Ethics*, which argues that infanticide is justified for up to 28 days after birth. In a concept he terms "total utilitarianism," Singer states that parents of a "defective" child ought to have the option of putting the child to death. He wrote, "Suppose that a newborn baby is diagnosed as a hemophiliac. The parents, daunted by the prospect of bringing up a child in this condition, are not anxious for him to live... the total view makes it necessary to ask whether the death of the hemophiliac infant would lead to the creation of another being who would not otherwise have existed. When the death of a disabled infant (one with hemophilia) will lead to the birth of another infant with better prospects of a happy life, the total amount of happiness will be greater if the disabled infant is killed. The loss of a happy life for the first infant is outweighed by the gain of a happier life for the second." Singer concludes, "The main point is clear: Killing a disabled infant is not morally equivalent to killing a person. Very often it is not wrong at all."

Rats, good. Sick babies, bad. Now, the indomitable Ivy League professor is at it again. In an article entitled, "Heavy Petting," which is a review of the book, *Dearest Pet: On Bestiality*, Singer proffers a thesis that is so revolting it has even been disavowed by many animal rights enthusiasts.

Singer's basic point is that the primary moral reason for not engaging in sex with animals is that such acts may be cruel to the animals — like rape. "But," he writes, "sex with animals does not always involve cruelty. Who has not been at a social occasion disrupted by the household dog gripping the legs of a visitor and vigorously rubbing its penis against them? The host usually discourages such activities, but in private not everyone objects to being used by her or his dog in this way, and occasionally mutually satisfying activities may develop."

It is almost beyond comprehension that Singer has offered a moral justification for bestiality. But indeed he does. In Singer's mind, animals are entitled to the same "pleasures" that human beings indulge in. Bestiality, therefore, is not an abomination in and of itself. This is equating sex with animals to one theory of sexual harassment in the office — it's only harassment if the woman takes offense and rejects you. If she's agreeable to the advance, it's... well, a date. Same with initiating sex with animals, according to Singer. If the goat finds it "mutually satisfying," who are human beings to deny the beast a good time?

Singer makes this point explicitly when he quotes author Midas Dekkers' historical account of how commonplace bestiality is. He includes sex with animals as simply part of a package of once-taboo sexual practices. "Not long ago," he writes, "any form of sexuality not leading to the conception of children was seen as, at best, wanton lust, or worse, a perversion. One by one, the taboos have fallen."

According to Singer, the taboo against bestiality has merely retained a more stubborn currency, and may likely fall one day. "Love for animals" has often been "thought of in ways that go beyond a pat and a hug." The normalcy Singer perceives in bestiality is best imparted by a story he relays of a woman visiting a camp of captured orangutans in Borneo. While walking through the camp, the woman was grabbed by an obviously aroused male orangutan.

Singer writes, "As it happened, the orangutan lost interest before penetration took place, but the aspect of the story that struck me most forcefully was that in the eyes of someone [the camp's proprietor] who has lived much of her life with orangutans, to be seen by one of them as an object of sexual interest is not a cause for shock or horror."

He continues, "The potential violence of the orangutan's come-on may have been disturbing, but the fact that it was an orangutan making the advances was not. That may be because... we are animals, indeed more specifically, we are great apes..." Singer then concludes his take on the orangutan's advance by stating that, "...it does imply that it ceases to be an offence to our status and dignity as human beings."

Singer's diatribe is so grotesque and graphic at times, that some of the more repulsive excerpts cannot be printed. But his general theme is consistent. On sex with hens, he objects because "it is usually fatal to the hen, and in some cases she will be deliberately decapitated just before ejaculation in order to intensify the convulsions of its sphincter." But, Singer adds in vintage "animal rights" logic, this cruelty is no worse than slaughtering hens for food.

The response to Singer's article has been shock and outrage, except for Ingrid Newkirk, the mindless president of the radical group PETA (People for the Ethical Treatment of Animals), whose response was, "It's daring and honest and it does not do what some people read into it, which is condone any violent acts involving an animal, sexual or otherwise... You know, Peter Singer is an intellectual, and he looks at all nuances of an issue." (Newkirk has also recently said she hopes the "foot and mouth" epidemic strikes America, as a way of getting even for America's cruelty to animals.)

In a subsequent statement released by PETA, they deny that they support bestiality, but state in part, "Dr. Singer was making the point that if we find things like that offensive, it should be because it's harmful to animals, and not because we humans are degraded by any association with animals. As always, Dr. Singer is concerned with showing that animals and humans share many traits, including the capacity for physical and psychological suffering. PETA agrees with Dr. Singer that it's time to recognize our similarities to animals, and work to improve the lives of all species."

Other animal rights groups, finally coming to their senses, were not so kind. Friends of Animals president Priscillia Feral finds "Singer's position shocking and disgusting." Program Coordinator Megan Metzellar says, "Singer has been put on a pedestal by the animal rights movement for a very long time but this essay is a wake-up call to those who have blindly idolized him."

Singer is tenured at Princeton, which has still not commented on his latest act of intellectual curiosity.

White Hypocrisy on Integration

There are so many instances of white liberal hypocrisy on racial matters that they cannot be easily enumerated. Certainly, whites who advocate affirmative action and racial preferences are never the first on line to give up their own jobs to the so-called "oppressed minorities" that they claim deserve redress for present and historical discrimination. In fact, these liberals are not even last on line. It is, frankly, a line they form for everyone else and from which they exempt themselves.

But the most transparent hypocrisy pertains to racial integration and diversity, which white liberals claim are vitally important and sources of great national strength, but from which they assiduously shield and disengage themselves and their families. Indeed, on no issue are fecklessness and dishonesty more evident than the myth of integration. *All* white liberals claim to believe in it, and *all* white liberals fail to practice it.

Americans have been so browbeaten into the politically correct thinking on integration, that even many Republicans and conservatives pretend they buy into the current orthodoxy, but none practice it. When reality hits home and Americans make decisions impacting their own lives -- housing, schools, jobs -- virtually all whites deliberately react in a perfectly natural manner and choose white institutions.

In a telephone survey conducted by Opinion Research International of Princeton, New Jersey, the question was asked, "Do you want to live in a neighborhood where your race is in the majority or one in which it is a minority?" White respondents -- by a proportion of 26 to one -- said that they wanted to live in a majority white neighborhood.

While people secretly know this is the obvious response and believe no survey need be taken to discover this answer, it is significant that so many whites were willing to openly say this on the telephone. Experts of all political persuasions agree that whites are usually notoriously dishonest in surveys of this kind and are inclined not to give the politically incorrect response. Perhaps the anonymity of the survey allowed whites to be more forthcoming about what is usually a latent, hidden sentiment.

(Hispanics answered that they preferred to live in a majority-Hispanic neighborhood by a four to one ratio, while blacks answered that they preferred living in a majority-black neighborhood by a slim eleven to eight ratio. These answers appear to be an acknoledgment that whites create the most desirable neighborhoods.)

All of this is in complete and hilarious contrast to what white public officials say, that integration is what everyone should want. This is the new American deception: public persons lie about wanting diversity and Americans pretend to believe them. As Don Feder of the *Boston Herald* writes, "The elite celebrate diversity; others have to live with it." Still another writer penned this clever commentary on elitist white liberal hypocrisy: "The purpose of a high education is to give people the right attitudes about minorities -- and the money to live as far away from them as possible."

Outside of public officials, the group most adamant about stressing integration and the vital importance of diversity are journalists. Investigative reporter Peter Brown of the *Orlando Sentinel* decided to survey the zip codes of 3,400 journalists to see where they lived. Surprise, surprise. He found that virtually all of them reside in upscale white neighborhoods, far from the non-whites they claim add "strength" to a locale. Brown found that more than one-third of *Washington Post* reporters live in just four white D.C. suburbs.

Paul Sperry, Washington Bureau Chief of WorldNetDaily.com, looked up two of the biggest journalistic promoters of racial integration, Chris Matthews, host of "Hardball" on CNBC and Ted Koppel, the long-time host of ABC's "Nightline." What prompted Sperry was Matthew's recent intonation that the evil of segregation still exists because the country is "run by white guys." As it happens, Matthews lives in Chevy Chase, Maryland, which is only five percent black.

Koppel, during a series on "Nightline" called, "America in Black and White," started off by hectoring some whites who live in a mostly-white area in Philadelphia. When they said they have some blacks in the neighborhood, Koppel responded with distress, "Six or seven out of 6,000. I mean it's a 99 percent white neighborhood." Koppel neglected to reveal he resides in lily-white Potomac, Maryland, which is also only five percent black.

The Clintons, of course, are the national cheerleaders for diversity. Among other various pronouncements, the President has said, "America is stronger because of... diversity, and the democracy we cherish flourishes in the great mosaic we have created since 1492." More recently, he said, "[Integration] is a matter of celebrating, relishing our differences... It'll make life more interesting."

Apparently, when choosing their own home, the Clintons preferred the boring and mundane, a domicile unworthy of celebration. They chose a house in segregated Chappaqua, New York, a neighborhood so white that the Clintons risk dying of homogeneity.

Professor Andrew Hacker, the Queens College sociologist and author of the 1992 bestseller, "Two Nations: Black and White, Separate and Unequal," is a white liberal who blames virtually all of black people's problems on whites. However misguided he may be, Hacker is nevertheless honest to a fault on white flight and housing patterns. He points out that whites of all political persuasions flee neighborhoods as they turn non-white. "I don't care care if one's left or right, when it comes down to it, we all behave as whites. The difference is that conservatives will admit that among themselves, while liberals hate having that view and wish they could get rid of it."

It is, of course, both a preposterous and a comical notion that a white person buying a home would ever do so in a black neighborhood. Chicago real estate brokers invented the term "white tax" as a way of describing how much more a house is worth simply because it exists in a white neighborhood, as opposed to an identical house in a black neighborhood. This "white tax" ranges anywhere from $50,000 to $100,000 and whites gladly pay it.

Despite white liberal hypocrites espousing the great wonders and benefits of integration and diversity, not one has come forward to lead by example, and none ever will.

When God Lived in New York

Thirty years ago this summer, while men were walking on the moon — bringing Walter Cronkite to tears, and while the most outrageous cultural gathering in history took place in the form of a weekend rock concert 30 miles from the town of Woodstock, New York, the greatest miracle of the 20th century was taking place in the friendly confines of Flushing, Queens.

"God is alive and well and living in an apartment in New York

City," said Tom Seaver, the ace pitcher of the New York Mets and now the team's announcer.

The Mets were born in 1962 in the shadow of the departed Brooklyn Dodgers and New York Giants and, of course, the despised Yankees. Their first manager was Yankee legend Casey Stengel, who said, "Come and see my amazing Mets, who in some cases have played only Triple-A ball." While Casey said this with a straight face, and the nickname has stuck with the team for 38 years, the fact of the matter was that the Mets were not "amazing" because they were good, but because they were so amazingly bad.

The Mets lost the first nine games they ever played and finished their inaugural season with a record-breaking 120 losses. The first four seasons in Met history all concluded with the team finishing in last place. In 1966, the Mets finally climbed out of last — finishing as high as ninth in the ten-team league. They sank back to last place in 1967 and then repeated their best finish ever in 1968 by improving once again to ninth. So in the team's first seven seasons, the Mets finished last five times and second-to-last the other two.

Heading into the 1969 season, the National League had expanded to twelve teams, thus creating two separate divisions, the East and the West. There was little reason to believe that the Mets would finish any higher than fifth, and even that would be in the second division. But the team played surprisingly well throughout the summer, staying relatively close to the heavily-favored Chicago Cubs, who were managed by the legendary Leo Durocher, former skipper of the Dodgers and Giants.

The Mets eventually faltered and on August 13th fell 13 and a half games behind the Cubs. When the Cubs invaded Shea Stadium for a three-game series, the event happened that is generally considered the turning point of the season. A black cat had gotten loose from underneath the stands. As timeout was called, the black cat slinked over to the front of the Cubs' dugout, stared menacingly at every player and then sauntered away. The Shea crowd went crazy. The Cubs were finished. The Mets went on a tear for the final six weeks and the team that had never finished higher than ninth, won its first division title in late September when the Cardinals' Joe Torre hit into the division-clinching double play.

The Mets would now play Hank Aaron's Atlanta Braves in the playoffs. Met pitcher Jerry Koosman said he was having nightmares about Aaron, and during these dreams Aaron had homered off him 45 straight times. When he finally faced Aaron in a real game, he struck him out the first time. Next time up, Aaron homered. He was 46 for 47. Nevertheless, the Mets swept the Braves and would face the powerful Baltimore Orioles of Brooks and Frank Robinson and Jim Palmer in the World Series, a team so awesome that they won their division by a whopping 21 games.

"Were the Mets a team of destiny?" one Baltimore sportswriter was asked. "Yes," he replied. "I think they are destined to be beaten badly by the Orioles."

After losing the first game in Baltimore, the Mets won game two by a 2-1 score on a home run by eventual Series Most Valuable Player, first baseman Donn Clendenon. Clendenon was asked after the game if he realized that his home run was the first time the Orioles had ever trailed in a post-season game. "Good," he said. "I hope they get used to it."

With the series tied 1-1 and heading back to Shea Stadium, Met centerfielder Tommie Agee led off Game 3 with a home run off Jim Palmer. Then Agee made two of the most incredible catches ever seen in the World Series, saving five runs alone with his glove and adding one more with his bat. Final score, 5-0 Mets.

Game Four saw the Mets take a 1-0 lead to the ninth inning behind Tom Seaver. As Seaver tired, the Orioles placed men on first and third with one out. The potential for a big inning loomed as the feared Brooks Robinson stepped to the plate. Robinson smashed a drive that was assured to be an extra-base hit which would give Baltimore the lead. Right fielder Ron Swoboda — always known as a poor fielder — dove to his right, making the most famous catch in World Series history. Although the game was now tied, the Shea crowd stood and cheered Swoboda's heroics. The Mets eventually won the game in the twelfth inning when pinch hitter J. C. Martin bunted to sacrifice but was hit by the throw. As the ball rolled into right field and the winning run scored, the Orioles were screaming that Martin was out of the baseline. But the ruling stood. The Mets were one win away from the impossible.

In 1969, all World Series games were still played during the day. Nuns interrupted classes so that the children could say a prayer for the Mets. Hippies who usually listened to rock music on their transistors were now tuning into the Mets.

Reality seemed to return in Game 5 as the Mets trailed 3-0 in the sixth inning. Cleon Jones led off and appeared to foul a ball off which rolled into the Mets dugout. Jones argued that he had been hit by the pitch and was entitled to first base. Mets manager Gil Hodges strolled from the dugout and produced the evidence: shoe polish on the ball! Jones was awarded first base. Clendenon followed with a 2-run homer. (Casey Stengel later told the press that the Mets always kept spare balls with shoe polish just in case.)

The next inning, the Mets' weakest hitter, Al Weis, stepped to the plate. Normally, his fly balls could barely reach the outfield. But this time he reached the fences. The game was tied. Everyone who remembers, knows that if Al Weis could hit a home run, there was no way the Mets could lose. They scored two runs in the eighth inning and the final out — which seemed to stay in the air forever — landed softly in Cleon Jones' glove. The miracle had come to pass... the Mets were World Champions.

At a time when America was enduring great strife both at home and abroad, the Mets provided proof that miracles do happen. Seaver was right. God was, indeed, a Met fan.

II

RACE AND GENETICS

For Whom the Bell Curve Tolls

Do the races differ in average intelligence? How definitive is the genetic component of these differences and to what degree does environment affect them? What exactly is intelligence and how is it measured? What are the unfiltered facts and evidence?

There was a time in America — very recently, in fact — when discussing racial differences in intelligence was the greatest intellectual crime one could commit. Although the facts were very well known by scientists and researchers, it was considered a suicidal career move to even address a topic of such a controversial nature. Much of that changed, however, with the release of *The Bell Curve* by Charles Murray and the late Richard Hernnstein in 1994. While the section in their book on racial differences in intelligence was comparatively small, and the data they imparted was neither original nor groundbreaking, the fact that such mainstream scholars went public with this information opened the doors to some serious discussion. Both the conservative *National Review* and the liberal *New Republic* kept an open mind on the subject and dedicated entire issues to it.

There are certainly some diehards — motivated by politics, not science — who refuse to acknowledge what virtually every informed scientist knows. But for the most part IQ differences in the races are so well-established that the only serious debate is *why* they exist, not if.

It is a fact that on average, blacks are one standard deviation (15 to 20 IQ points) less intelligent than whites. Whites, on the other hand, are on average five points less intelligent than north Asians. The most important words in these axioms are "on average." Obviously, there are many very intelligent black people who are smarter than many whites and Asians. But, "on average," blacks are less intelligent. While political dogma has denied this fact for a generation or two, no one with the slightest grasp of the data questions it. This is similar to pointing out that men "on average" are taller than women. Everyone knows this. Of course, there are some women that are taller than some men, but this does not change the averages.

Intelligence has not always been the easiest thing to define to everyone's liking. But there have certainly been many standardized tests which have proven spectacularly accurate in measuring IQ. So accurate have they been, that tracking people's performance over a lifetime has borne out the value of intelligence testing. Indeed, the races consistently show the same results wherever they are tested in the world. They do so stubbornly and consistently.

Even people uninitiated in science understand that intelligence is to a very large degree set at birth and is the crucial measuring stick as to whether a person will be successful in life. IQ tests began during World War I and for nearly 80 years the results have not changed. The racial gap in scores remains constant.

Black Americans have an average IQ of 85. Whites average 100 and north Asians average 105. These numbers have not deviated despite every superhuman effort to see that they do. Civil rights laws, expanded opportunities, affirmative action, Head Start and trillions of dollars aimed at lifting blacks have not made a dent in black IQ scores. Yet these are not the only stark realities that suggest that intelligence is genetic in origin and that the races differ in intelligence. Precise and elaborate testing — adoption studies whereby black infants were raised in upper middle-class white homes by high-IQ parents — always produced IQ's in the children which mirrored their *biological* parents, eliminating the possibility that somehow environment is responsible for IQ.

No one disputes that environment plays a part in intelligence, but it plays a very small part. Scientists now estimate that only 15 to 20 percent of IQ is impacted by environment. Therefore, it is not the often squalid conditions in which blacks live that *cause* low IQ. Quite the opposite. Those conditions are the *result* of low intelligence.

Only 16 percent of blacks have IQ's of over 100, which is the white average. Whites are six to eight times more likely than blacks to have scores in the "gifted" range of 135 or higher. Blacks are six to eight times more likely than whites to have scores in the "retarded" range of 70 or lower. Blacks, moreover, are virtually non-existent at the highest, "genius" level of IQ.

American blacks, who on average possess 25 percent white genes, are the most intelligent blacks in the world. According to Professor Richard Lynn of the University of Ulster in Ireland, the average IQ in black Africa — peopled by pure blacks — is much lower. The average IQ in Uganda and Ghana is 80; in Nigeria it is 75; and in Zaire the average IQ is 65. These facts go a long way to explaining the backwardness of sub-Saharan Africa. The 1914 edition of the Encyclopedia Brittanica noted matter-of-factly that, "The Negro is intellectually inferior to the Caucasian." While such bluntness is too caustic for today's sensibilities, the matter of racial differences was suppressed until 1994 for totally non-intellectual reasons.

Many of these facts are uncomfortable for many people. Criticisms of these realities are often based on emotion, anger and politics. But Einstein said, "Condemnation without investigation is the height of ignorance."

Heterodox: Nature Trumps Nurture

There was a time when the debate over racial differences in IQ focused on whether or not those differences exist at all. Ever since Prof. Arthur Jensen of the University of California at Berkeley authored his landmark article, "How Much Can We Boost IQ and Achievement?" in 1969, so-called experts have tried to discredit his findings. All have failed.

The line of defense for reckless egalitarians moved backward. Virtually no egalitarian for several years wanted to admit that the races differ in average intelligence quotient, but the numbers were indisputable. What detractors of these truths then necessarily needed to argue was that, yes, there are differences in the test scores that haven't changed since testing began in World War I, but the tests must be meaningless. Blacks scored lower, they asserted, because the tests were "culturally biased." How could blacks be expected to score as high on a test devised by whites?

This desperate attempt to shun reality ignored two obvious points. First, north Asians, who speak no English and could hardly claim to hold a leg up on blacks on American culture, not only outscored blacks every time, but on average outscored whites. Mexicans, American Indians, Polynesians, Micronesians, Melanesians and Maoris also outscored blacks. Secondly, no test has ever been devised where blacks scored as high as whites. The average racial differences in IQ have persisted throughout the creation of every conceivable IQ test.

Moreover, if indeed the tests were biased against blacks, then logically the scores would underpredict black ability. The tests could be dismissed if blacks consistently outperformed in whatever it is the tests predicted they would do. Alas, this does not happen. The scores are stubbornly accurate as to black performance.

As common as the charge of test bias is, it is nothing more than an *ex post facto* claim. The tests *must have been* biased simply because blacks didn't do well and egalitarians dislike the results. Specific bias on a specific test question has never actually been found. In fact, most modern IQ tests, such as Raven's Progressive Matrices, have no verbal or cultural content at all. They merely test a person's understanding of shapes and patterns. Others involve reaction-time and speed. Believers in test bias cannot explain why a test has never been invented which eliminated it. It has not been for lack of trying.

The great irony is that those tests which involve language and inevitably contain some cultural content (and theoretically could be biased) are those in which the black/white gap is *narrowest*. The more culturally specific an intelligence test is, the narrower the gap becomes. The most abstract, culture-free tests reveal the largest differences in the racial gap.

Having lost the "test bias" argument badly, egalitarians then resorted to the "environmental" argument. Yes, they concede, these tests accurately measure intelligence and, yes, blacks on average are less intelligent than whites. But, this is all due to environment, they claim, not genetics. The often and historically squalid conditions in which blacks live account for low intelligence. Thus, the nature vs. nurture debate.

The evidence for genetic rather than environmental causes for intelligence is more than overwhelming. Even former proponents of the environmental theory, scientists such as Stephen Jay Gould, Leon Kamin and Richard Lewontin, have fallen strangely silent. There is no longer any informed opinion which takes the environmental point of view, although there are still some staggering remnants of *uninformed* opinion. The scientific consensus of 661 recognized authorities in education and psychological testing concluded that intelligence is profoundly heritable.

Of all the evidence supporting the genetic origin of intelligence, the most telling comes from twin studies. Identical twins have exactly the same genes. When they are separated at birth and reared apart they still grow to have virtually identical IQ's, even though they were raised in different environments.

Fraternal twins are no more genetically similar than ordinary siblings. Reared in the same family, they have environments that are as similar as possible, yet the gap in the IQ's of fraternal twins (or other siblings) raised together is greater than the gap for identical twins raised apart. This has been proven by many exhaustive twin studies. Identical genes simply count for more than identical environments.

Similar studies have been done on the race and IQ question. The Minnesota Transracial Adoption Study found that black infants raised by white college graduates had IQ's of 89 by age 17; babies that were mixed race (half white-half black) had IQ's of 98; and the all-white controls had IQ's of 106. All of these results revealed that race and heritability were virtually unaffected by the change in environment. Ironically, the 18 year study was originally commenced in order to *disprove* the genetic and racial take on intelligence.

Further demolishing the now-discredited environmental theory is the fact that black students who are raised in families with incomes of more than $70,000 per year get lower scores on IQ and aptitude tests than whites raised in homes with incomes of less than $20,000 per year, including whites below poverty level.

Much of this, while scientifically documented, is still heterodox to many. But it is simply common sense to the casual observer. Intelligent people tend to have intelligent children. An expensive house does not raise someone's IQ. But a high IQ will make it more likely that someone will own an expensive house. Nature does indeed trump nurture.

Why It Matters

A caller to a recent radio program opined, "The scientific evidence supporting the view that the races differ in average intelligence is well-established and accurate. But the subject should be ignored because it only results in hurt feelings."

When Professor Michael Levin was victorious in court on First Amendment grounds after his City College colleagues censured and censored his right to express his views on race and intelligence, some observers, while conceding that Levin's views were correct and that City College had mistreated him, nevertheless felt that Levin had brought his problems upon himself for even broaching such a sensitive topic.

Indeed, there is a strain of thought that believes discussion of racial differences in intelligence — acknowledging that blacks on average are one standard deviation (15 IQ points) less intelligent than whites — is so incendiary, that people should simply leave it alone.

This mindset is misguided and erroneous for two basic reasons. First, the truth should never be suppressed, especially when it involves free and open scientific inquiry. In a society that prides itself on the First Amendment, there should always be a presumption in favor of the truth. Democracy, in fact, is said to *require* the truth. Thomas Jefferson said, "There is not a truth existing which I fear, or would wish unknown to the whole world." Therefore, the censors of the world are revealing their ignorance — and cowardice — by attempting to silence the likes of Michael Levin for discussing a truth they find unacceptable.

Herbert Spencer wrote that the greatest of infidelities was the fear that the truth may be bad. Mark Twain said, "Nothing astonishes people more than to tell them the truth." Of course, as has been pointed out, people do not always react with relief and gratitude when the truth is revealed to them. They often become attached to their illusions and resent having unpleasant truths foist upon them. They would, in fact, rather wallow in their own ignorance with their angry demeanor and that very sturdy chip on their shoulder.

The second, and ultimately more important reason for a frank discussion of race and intelligence, is the level of injustice that is inflicted upon Americans by their government which enacts policies predicated on the fallacious view that these differences don't exist. On average, blacks score lower on every conceivable aptitude test than whites and Asians. These tests include everything from IQ tests to college admissions exams to police sergeant promotion tests to sanitation entry exams. These results have not changed despite decades of heroic efforts to uplift blacks to and to tinker with the tests.

But rather than acknowledge what every (yes, *every*) study and informed scientist has put forth, the government's official position is that blacks fall short because of white wickedness. Oppression and discrimination by whites are responsible, not inherent shortcomings. (Asians, who outperform whites, have a significant history of discrimination in America, but that's an inconvenient fact.) The government makes, as its official rationale for discriminating against whites and Asians through affirmative action, quotas, set-asides and favoritism, a policy which denies that there are racial differences in intelligence. That is, a policy *which has no basis in fact or for which there is no evidence.*

Therefore, a frank acknowledgment of the truth regarding these differences would completely destroy the very basis for policies that have hurt people's lives. Should someone of a particular race obtain a job or a promotion even though he scored lower on the qualifying exam? Is that justice? Well, yes, as long as the government continues to spout the nonsense that the lower scores are due to oppression rather than natural ability.

Try explaining to an economically poor white or Asian why they were passed over for a job or promotion although they scored highest. Try also explaining that the reason for this injustice is that the upper middle class black who got the job was chosen because he is "oppressed."

Of course, the liberals who wail about this sordid discussion are never the ones who sacrifice their own jobs or the opportunities of their own children to promote this grotesque "justice" for the so-called "oppressed." The old joke that "a conservative is a liberal who has been mugged" plays out perfectly here. Until one is affected by the government's scurrilous policy of refusing to acknowledge these racial differences, it is easy to sit back and defend the laws that are mistreating certain Americans.

The American government and the ivory tower elitists who defend the laws of discrimination through affirmative action have sentenced many Americans to injustice. Those laws have never worked and will never work because they refuse to acknowledge nature. Acknowledging the truth about differences in intelligence is the only way to ensure that all people will be treated fairly. *That's why it matters.* Let the chips fall where they may.

"Drive out nature with a pitchfork," wrote the Roman satirist Juvenal, "and it will nevertheless return."

No Quotas Needed in Sports

If the principles of affirmative action were applied to professional sports, and teams were required to hire by racial quotas instead of on pure talent and ability, American fans would be watching a bunch of clowns on the field and on the court.

Blacks are 12 percent of the American population, yet comprise over 80 percent of the players in the National Basketball Association and roughly two-thirds of the players in the National Football League. Blacks dominate these sports despite the fact that whites are just as interested as blacks in becoming professional athletes. There are more whites in college football and basketball than there are in the pros because whites simply don't have what it takes to compete at the pro level in the same numbers as blacks.

Since whites outnumber blacks six to one in the general population, an equivalent number of each race on the professional level would still make blacks proportionately dominant. But with blacks vastly outnumbering whites in the pro ranks, black excellence can only be characterized as breathtaking.

Not only do blacks dominate football and basketball, but also boxing, with the last white heavyweight champion being Ingemar Johansson -- some 40 years ago.

In any skill involving speed, whites are virtually nonexistent. There are 30 teams in the NFL, which means there are 60 starting running backs, 60 starting cornerbacks, 60 starting wide receivers and 120 starting defensive backs. Last season, 58 of 60 running backs were black; 59 of 60 wide receivers were black; 117 of 120 defensive backs were black, as were *all 60 cornerbacks*. (Jason Sehorn of the Giants returns this year, making him the only white starting cornerback.) In positions involving strength, like the offensive line, whites are much more represented. A white wide receiver or running back has not totaled 1,000 yards in rushing or receiving since 1986.

Even going back in NFL history when white receivers were more prevalent, the great ones such as Lance Alworth and Fred

Belitnikoff were more known for their great hands than for speed.

In baseball, blacks lead both leagues in stolen bases every year. The last white to do it was probably Ty Cobb.

At the Olympics, the 100 meter dash is simply a competition between blacks. Not one white, Asian, Arab or Hispanic even qualified for the final. All eight finalists were West Africans. So when the United States competes with Great Britain or Canada in these events, it is nothing more than a test to see which country has the faster black man. All sprinting events are simply blacks against blacks.

Black dominance is so stark that *every medal* in the men's 100m, 200m, 400m, 110m hurdles, and the gold in the 4 x 100m and 4 x 400m relays went to blacks. And black prowess in the long jump is even more overwhelming than in the sprints.

The blacks who dominate these events, as well as American black athletes, are almost exclusively of West African descent. In long distances, it is blacks who also win, but it is East Africans who do so. East Africans won the gold in the 800m, 1,500m, 3,000m steeplechase, 5,000m, 10,000m and the marathon. In the World Cross-Country Championships, the first ten finishers were all from Kenya or Ethiopia.

Kenyans have won the *last nine* World Championships. Kenyans also won the 800m, 1,500m, 3,000m steeplechase and the 5,000m. Based on population percentages, the likelihood of this happening is one in 1.6 billion!

Clearly, only natural ability can account for these incredible performances. No amount of training can overcome such innate skills.

But the natural factor in black skills is even more pronounced than it seems. West Africans and East Africans excel in separate domains, with virtually no overlap. No East African has ever won an Olympic sprint. No West African has ever won a medal at a distance of greater than 800 meters. All 29 Olympic distance medals went to East Africans, with 27 of them going to Kenyans and Ethiopians alone. West Africans win all the sprints.

What accounts for such black dominance? Anyone who has

ever played sports on any level knows that no amount of training can compensate for natural ability, especially when it comes to speed. You're either fast or you aren't. *Runner's World* magazine lists the characteristics that have been found to separate blacks of West African descent from whites.

"Blacks have less body fat, narrower hips, thicker thighs, longer legs and lighter calves. From a biomechanical perspective, this is an impressive package. Narrow hips allow for efficient, straight-ahead running. Strong quadriceps muscles provide horsepower, and light calves reduce resistance."

According to *Runner's World*, blacks also have proportionately more "fast-twitch" muscle fiber than whites, which gives explosive power, as opposed to slow-twitch muscles, which give the steady contractions needed in swimming and rowing (where whites dominate.)

When natural ability and skill are allowed to dictate who wins and loses, all's fair. If only the same principles were applied throughout society as those applied in sports. Let the best man win.

Taboo: Why Blacks Dominate Sports

Violations of racial orthodoxy are so rare in contemporary America, that even incremental steps in combatting the establishment line can only be welcome. The supreme premise on which all other facets of racial madness rest is the nonsensical notion that all races are symmetrically equal in all ways. Deep down, everyone knows this is untrue. But racial dogma is scarcely informed by truth.

It is an irrefutable fact that blacks dominate sports, not only in the United States, but around the world. In virtually all sporting events involving running and jumping, the only competition blacks face is from other blacks. If the United States were to compete with, say, England in a variety of track meets, the event would simply be a contest to see which nation has the fastest African within its borders. Such a competition would merely show in which country the fastest black man lives. Even in baseball — a sport not generally considered dominated by blacks — blacks are overrepresented.

It borders on grotesque silliness watching people deny the obvious. The average black person knows it's true, as does the average white person. It is black activists and so-called spokespeople (those who should disdainfully be referred to as Professional Blacks) who fall all over themselves denying it.

Whites in public life, who for the most part live in absolute terror of Professional Blacks and take their cue from them, function as bestial censors regarding these racial discussions.

Why would an axiom that on the surface appears to be praising blacks, be regarded as so offensive? There are basically two reasons: First, it is assumed that lurking somewhere deep in the recesses of the notion of black athletic superiority is the corollary that what blacks have in physical ability, they lack in brains. This, of course, exceeds all limits of racial paranoia. Bob Herbert, a Professional Black who writes editorials for the *New York Times*, wrote that praising blacks for their athleticism is "a genteel way to say nigger." Another *New York Times* story quotes another black decrying scientific investigation of race and athletics as "an underhanded way" of saying "blacks are closer to beast... than they are to the rest of humanity." Please. Legendary sports writer Frank Deford counters these arguments by stating, "... when Jack Nicklaus sinks a 30-foot putt, nobody thinks his IQ goes down." Likewise, the great Alan Page, an MVP black defensive tackle from the 1960's and 70's, must have been kept in the dark on all this when he became a circuit court judge.

The second reason discussion of black athletic superiority is frowned upon is that any inquiry into racial differences is simply regarded as an off-limits subject. The fear is in what else might be found.

Now along comes Jon Entine with his book, "Taboo: Why Black Athletes Dominate Sports and Why We're Afraid to Talk About It." Entine is an Emmy-winning producer for NBC and ABC

News and has also won a National Press Club Award. Back in 1988 Entine first became a denizen of racial controversy when he wrote and produced an NBC documentary with Tom Brokaw entitled, "Black Athletes: Fact and Fiction." It was the same year Jimmy "the Greek" Snyder was fired for praising black athletes as having been "bred" to physical excellence. NBC, Brokaw and Entine all deserved credit for seeking and expounding on the truth. But some truths, the Thought Police say, are to be buried, distorted, denied and ignored.

The basic premise in "Taboo" is that there are obvious physiological and genetic reasons why blacks excel in sports. This is so apparent that in a sane world it would be nothing more than a curiosity. It is only in an *insane* world that these discussions become objects of scorn, hysteria and censorship. No one, for example, disputes that genetics determine susceptibility to sickle-cell anemia (which affects blacks) or Tay-Sachs disease (which inordinately affects Jews), as well as prostate cancer, diabetes and osteoporosis. Races differ in susceptibility to all of these diseases.

The concentration of certain races to particular athletic performances is so precise and overwhelming that only fanatic egalitarians can doubt its existence. In sprints of up to 400 meters, West Africans win all the events. After that distance, the races are all won by East Africans. There is no overlap whatsoever. Coincidence? Chance? Of course not. In fact, in the long distance races, Kenyans dominate among the East Africans. And one particular group, the Kalenjin, win 70 percent of Kenya's gold medals. The chances of this happening by coincidence are literally in the billions. The Kalenjins themselves laugh at the idea that the answer is anything other than genetic.

Simply put, the correlates of black supremacy in athletics are confirmed by hundreds of studies. Blacks possess the natural physical makeup to excel in sports: on average, longer arms and legs, shorter trunk, narrower hips, less body fat and a larger percentage of "fast-twitch" muscle fiber, which is essential for explosive bursts of speed. West Africans also have a lower lung capacity than East Africans, which is why they wear out in long distances and why there are no black championship swimmers. "Taboo" also points out that blacks need less time for training.

In the end, Jon Entine has provided a much-needed public service, by attaching his award-winning name to an issue that cries out for frank discussion. A leading black scholar and author, Earl Smith of Wake Forest University, wrote Entine, "You will be accused of spouting old fashioned racism for even raising the issue of African American superiority in athletics." And so he has, but not at the expense of producing a book that is both irrefutable and long overdue.

Wanted: Black Organ Donors

Last month, the great Hall of Fame running back Walter Payton, the all-time leading rusher in football history, died of kidney disease at the age of 44. Six months earlier, Payton shocked the nation with his tearful admission that only a kidney transplant could save him. Despite the feeling that the rich and famous receive special treatment, the kidney never came.

There may have been innumerable reasons why Payton died, and certainly there was no guarantee that an organ transplant would have saved him. Nevertheless, the lack of black participation in medical research and blacks' reluctance to donate organs is becoming a not-so-well-guarded secret. Proportionately, blacks are much less likely than whites to donate organs, give blood or volunteer in any way to benefit medical research.

It is a scientific fact that the compatibility of organs is much greater *within* a particular race than *between* races. Thus, when blacks refuse to act as potential donors, the lives lost are almost certainly those of other blacks. This non-willingness to donate on the part of blacks will undoubtedly result in more Walter Paytons. Yet black shunning of these life-giving activities exists despite intensive recruitment efforts to get blacks involved in medical research, even on the part of black churches. And in response to the nonsensical view that medical science somehow ignores nonwhites, the National Institutes of Health and other grant-making bodies now mandate that biological research include a discernible number of minority research subjects. It is usually an effort in futility.

Why are blacks such reluctant medical subjects? There appear to be several answers. The evidence for some reasons is largely anecdotal and speculative — maybe even dubious — but they are discussed in *The Scientist*, a prestigious life sciences newspaper. *The Scientist* bemoans the fact that blacks are uncooperative subjects for crucial medical research and has sought to explain why. The people *The Scientist* interviewed almost uniformly feel that science is overly "white" and blacks need to be recruited as scientists, which would then make blacks feel more comfortable about volunteering for medical research.

But the more standard explanation offered is the infamous Tuskegee syphilis experiment. In the 40 year study, which ended in 1972, American government scientists charted the progress of syphilis in 400 Alabama black men who were deliberately left untreated in order for doctors to study the disease as it ran its course. Although this is the only known instance of government medical malfeasance, Tuskegee has come to symbolize the wickedness of white medical research and its deadly, unfeeling hostility toward blacks.

The Scientist also reports that blacks simply do not trust government medical research because so many of them adhere to the preposterous view that the AIDS virus was created in a laboratory in order to conduct genocide against blacks. Fully one-third of American blacks either believe this or believe that it is likely.

Another explanation for black non-participation in *The Scientist* is the notion that blacks do not have "equal access" to medicine. James Bowman, a black professor of medicine at the University of Chicago, says, "As long as we have an inequitable health care system, minorities must be suspicious. If they're not, they're foolish." Kathleen Boozang, a Seton Hall University professor (whose race is not given) continues along this line. "If you're asked to be a subject of research, but then aren't going to reap the benefits, why should you participate?" she asks.

A black female genetics counselor explains that blacks fear science in general because of books like "The Bell Curve," [which says] "we're inferior. You have scientists or even educators saying this."

Somehow, none of these reasons seem to quite fully explain blacks' mistrust and apathy toward the medical community. Even when the research involves diseases like prostate cancer or hypertension — afflictions which strike at blacks at a higher rate than other races — blacks show no more of a propensity to participate. The situation has become so dire that black churches have been enlisted to recruit potential volunteers. Still, scientists have become disheartened upon realizing that many black preachers expect to be paid for providing willing churchgoers. One preacher said, "If you want to change a church's agenda to fit something on your own agenda, you need to invest in the infrastructure of the church." Not exactly the selfless attitude one might expect.

One black breast cancer activist blames the poor judgement of the recruiters who foolishly send a white person instead of a black into the black community looking for volunteers. She says, "The congregation is very polite, but the people have no intention of complying."

In the end, it may be nothing more than a cultural characteristic that keeps blacks from involving themselves in medical research. Whites ordinarily don't volunteer solely on the belief that they will personally benefit. And while the high black crime rate may serve as an indicator for a general contempt for society, the rate differential in research participation transcends even this category. Non-criminal blacks with high incomes still volunteer at a much lower rate than whites.

Finally, superstitions and non-scientific explanations for disease are much more prevalent among blacks than whites. It is astounding how much space is occupied in black newspapers by psychics, faith healers, numerology books, good luck charms and other such nonsense. A community which places so much faith in faith healers rather than the biological origins of disease probably won't harbor much interest in medical research.

The Biological Reality of Race

Paranoia and general uneasiness concerning matters of race has led to the bizarre and unscientific axiom that race is merely a "social construct," a man-made phenomenon that has no legitimate place in pragmatic application. Race, the deniers assert, is only "skin deep."

Fanatical social egalitarians are the most adamant proponents of the notion that race doesn't exist. They even delve into the realm of biology in order to buttress their claim, completely unaware it seems, that the science of biology and genetics provides more than ample evidence of the reality of race.

All of this nonsense began when liberals sought to follow the utopian communist model, which maintained that all people were symmetrically equal. In their quest to create a "fair and just" society, the political left dismissed biological evidence and concluded that all differences in class and achievement necessarily were the result of oppression. Hence, programs like affirmative action were created from the mistaken assumption that racial disparities in achievement were the result of white wickedness, not inherent ability. The programs would, therefore, discriminate against whites in order to achieve not equality of opportunity, but equality of *results*. It is this corrupted premise from which all racial madness in America stems.

The one area in which race is not denied is in physical appearance. Even liberals don't pretend that they can't tell the difference between members of different races. What they do assert is that outside of the external cosmetic, differences are simply in the minds of bad people.

They go so far as to cite alleged scientific evidence to prove their point. One argument maintains that because human beings of different races are 99.9 percent genetically similar, there can be no race differences and no races. It is quite true that human populations share roughly 99.9 percent of their genes. But to conclude from this that there is no such thing as race assumes that significant differences cannot be extracted from 0.1 percent of genetic differences. The fact is that even what appears to be an irrelevant genetic difference can have a profound variation in reality.

For example, human beings share 98 percent of their genes with chimpanzees, yet no one would maintain that such a small variation in genetic makeup means chimpanzees are equal to humans. Furthermore, humans share nearly as high a percentage of genetic similarity with mice and dogs. That is because most genes produce basic body structures that all mammals have in common. What appear to be small differences can make all the change in the world. It is a biological fact that large differences in organisms are caused by very small differences in genes. What this all proves is that verifiable genetic differences in races are very significant indeed.

To further illustrate this point, sex differences between men and women are the result of just one gene, referred to as the Testes Determining Factor. All species have 50,000 to 100,000 genes. Therefore, men and women are 99.998 to 99.999 percent genetically identical, yet no one claims that sex is merely a "social construct."

Differences between human races are analogous to differences in breeds of dogs, which mathematically appear to be very small. But it is obvious that a Doberman pinscher differs in every conceivable way from a dachshund. Dog breeds differ in temperament, behavior, intelligence and, of course, appearance. The genetic percentage of similarity between Dobermans and dachshunds is, therefore, the same as between blacks, whites and North Asians. Furthermore, butterflies and caterpillars are 100 percent genetically identical, which demonstrates that a .01 percent genetic difference can cause an almost unrecognizable variation.

An offshoot of this first erroneous argument by the race deniers is similar and just as misplaced. They state that there is more genetic variation *within* groups than between them. So, they conclude, this again proves that race differences are invalid.

Again, this assertion, while technically true, does not lead to the conclusion the egalitarians point to. There is, for example, considerable variation between siblings or between parents and children. No one would deny, however, that siblings and parents are more closely related to each other than to strangers. The same holds true for races. While two given black people, for example, may have genetic differences with each other, that does not disprove the fact that they are still more closely related to each other than they are to a white or North Asian person.

It is only when liberals see an advantage in recognizing race that they acknowledge its existence. In the same sentence, and with a straight face, a radical egalitarian can deny the existence of race when genetic factors prove differences in achievement and ability, then assert racial consciousness when claiming spoils such as affirmative action, preferences and set-asides.

III

POLITICS AND GOVERNMENT

Race Commission Report a Farce

After fifteen predictably unproductive months, the orchestrated monologue that has purported to be an independent, open-minded advisory panel has released its "findings." With White House fanfare as a backdrop, President Clinton's appointed commission on race has reported that "White Privilege" continues to exist in America. It also found that affirmative action should continue; racial stereotyping in media should be studied; criminal sentences for crack and cocaine use should be reduced because non-whites disproportionately indulge in those drugs; racial profiling (the use of race to determine profiles of criminal suspects) should be re-thought; civil rights laws should be more strictly enforced and a permanent body should be created to further study and promote racial dialogue and harmony.

In addition, the panel laments the "continuing existence of prejudice and privilege" and states that an apology for slavery is "much too narrow" a solution. "It is, we believe, essential, to recall the facts of racial domination..." the final report advises. What a surprise.

This entire fiasco began in June of 1997 when, in a speech at the University of California at San Diego, Bill Clinton announced his grand plans to unleash a presidential initiative on race, with an advisory panel chaired by black historian John Hope Franklin. In the most truthful statement he has ever made in three decades of public life, Clinton said about race, "People have held back in private discussions. That duplicity has to end because there are ideas and convictions about race that must be challenged and changed, and neither can happen unless there is an honest laying on the table of what we all believe and think."

Regrettably — and predictably — Clinton never really intended such straightforward honesty about the third rail of American social and political life. Officially named "One America in the 21st

Century: The President's Initiative on Race," the commission was a farce from the start. It was laughable to even entertain the notion that the panel might conclude that affirmative action was failed and misguided. Likewise, it was preposterous to consider that the commission would give serious thought to reconsidering the disastrous integrationist imperative. Everyone knew, despite the commission's town hall meetings, televised discussions and other facades implying seriousness, that this entire endeavor was a bad and pre-determined joke.

A serious analysis of race could not possibly conclude that all the failed policies of the past forty years be continued, but alas, this was not a serious analysis. Despite the President's stated goal of "candid dialogue," the commission did nothing but spout the same tired bromides about white wickedness, white guilt and white culpability. From the start, the initiative was seen as a transparent charade.

In November, when the panel announced that it would not include any criticism of affirmative action, even the liberal American Jewish Congress was furious. Phil Baum, AJC's executive director, said, "If the presidential panel wants to talk only to itself, fine. But then don't pretend that it is a 'dialogue' and don't try to pass off its findings as a serious review of the possibilities."

Indeed, there was more of an honest exchange of different ideas on the old Soviet Politburo than in this sham of a commission. With this type of stinging criticism even from its allies, the panel began pretending to take input from so-called "conservatives" like William Bennett, who despite questioning affirmative action, never challenged the panel's basic premises.

And those basic premises are the same discredited assumptions that have comprised racial orthodoxy in America for decades, never to be questioned, always to be accepted as gospel: the failings of non-whites are the fault of white racism; all races share the same level of abilities and only white treachery prevents equality of results; justice is defined as equal results, not equal opportunity; Americans want racial integration in their own lives and such integration is inherently a good thing; racial diversity is a source of strength.

All of these assumptions, of course, are false. Deep down, moreover, everyone knows they are false. A serious and candid discussion of race would have begun with a public repudiation of these falsehoods. The answers to the tough questions would then flow more easily and truthfully. Why is there so much black crime? What really causes the phenomenon of "white flight"? Is it really white ignorance or an honest desire to live in a safe neighborhood with good schools? Why is affirmative action nothing more than discrimination against whites? Why do Asians succeed where blacks fail? Why do whites sit back in silence while blacks remove George Washington's name from public schools? Why does racial diversity always result in strife, bitterness and antagonisms, when it is claimed to be a "strength"? If diversity is such a strength, why do whites always avoid it in their own lives?

The farcical nature of the President's commission on race is merely a reflection of the severe limits of expression on America's most daunting problem. Until the veil of dogma is lifted, Americans will know they are being snookered by bogus "initiatives" and their predictable "findings."

What Head Start?

As expected, the Republican-controlled Congress, with knees shaking in fear and trepidation, acquiesced and abandoned professed principles (again), passing a pork-laden budget which included the restoration of funding for the sacred cow Head Start program.

Of all the disastrous social programs emerging from the 1960's, Head Start actually enjoys the best reputation. There has never been any evidence of its success, but the official word is that it works, so who are the Republicans to dare to oppose that proposition? Those who cheerlead for Head Start, naturally, are those who implement it. Beware of people who push for renewed and increased funding for a program on which — by the strangest coincidence — their jobs depend.

Head Start was originally created for the purpose of providing educational, social and health services to disadvantaged children on the premise that low minority test scores and lower levels of achievement were due purely to environmental factors. Create a more favorable environment and it will be proven that intelligence and achievement levels will even out, the theory goes.

After 30 years, 15 million children served and $30 billion spent, a generous view of Head Start would be that its effectiveness is inconclusive, with no sure results as to its performance. In a five-year strategic plan on Head Start submitted to Congress in September, 1997, the Department of Health and Human Services could not describe what the program was supposed to accomplish. According to Nina H. Shokraii and Patrick F. Fagan of the Heritage Foundation, "Scant amount of useful research exist to evaluate Head Start" and "the vast amount of research, including that cited as proof of the program's effectiveness by Head Start, was methodologically suspect or antiquated."

They base these conclusions on the General Accounting Office's report that research on Head Start provides little information on the program's impact. It states, "The most reliable way to determine program impact is to compare a group of Head Start participants with an equivalent group of non-participants..." The report remarks that this was only done once and its findings were inconclusive.

All of this, although clearly a non-endorsement of Head Start, is actually giving the program the benefit of the doubt. Neither Shokraii and Fagan nor the GAO report explicitly states that Head Start has failed (although they strongly imply that it has.) A more accurate view, however, offers that the program has indeed failed at its most elementary purpose — to boost achievement *in perpetuity* and verify the idea that achievement levels are not hereditary, but environmental.

The entire subject of intelligence being linked to genes, heredity and race is too hot a political topic for most to handle. Orthodoxy maintains that race and genes don't matter when it comes to intelligence. All reliable studies suggest otherwise. Those factors not only matter, they are definitive. So when programs like Head Start fail, it becomes rather embarrassing to expose why. Even opponents of the program are reluctant to discuss the innate intelligence factor, so results that reveal the importance of genes and race to intelligence (and the relative non-importance of environment) are conveniently buried.

A typical Head Start program assumes that if, for example, a poor black child's early environment is enriched, his achievement will equal that of a middle class white child's and, because of this "head start" which has leveled the playing field, the child's IQ will reach its full potential — again, equal to that of the white child.

The Milwaukee Project, the most thorough long-term study of such a program, was undertaken in the 1980's at a cost of millions of dollars. A group of infants was chosen to spend five days a week in "infant stimulation centers" which had greatly enriched environments. The children were kept in the program for six years and then sent to regular public schools. Amidst great public fanfare, it was reported triumphantly that these children did indeed score 30 points higher on IQ tests than a control group.

What was not reported was that three years later, the academic levels of achievement for the "enriched" group were found to be indistinguishable from those of the control group raised in poverty. Innate intelligence levels were also found to be the same — averaging about an IQ of 80. Of course, the IQ's of these children never really "dropped" because intelligence does not really change. What the study proved was that achievement levels can be artificially boosted in the very short term. The most significant result of the Milwaukee Project was the fact that the gains achieved through Head Start enrichment *did not last.* Pure intelligence was shown to be genetic after all.

A more recent study conducted by J.S. Fuerst of Loyola University tracked 684 black children placed in a program so enriched he dubbed it "Head Start to the fourth power." The children's test scores significantly surpassed those of the control group. But ten years after the enriched group returned to regular schools, its performance mirrored ordinary children.

Reality reveals that performance levels cannot be maintained. When "enriched" students are then mistakenly placed in "advanced" classes, the gap between the truly intelligent and the artificially boosted students widens. Educators then fall all over themselves trying to explain this away while creating a "dumbed down" curriculum in order to narrow the achievement gap. So a "head start" for some results in a handicap for others.

Health Care: Government is the Problem

Americans have been so successfully brainwashed into thinking that government can or should solve all their ills, that they readily look to government to remedy problems which government caused in the first place. Brezhnev once said socialism was irreversible and to a large extent he was right. Once weaned on the public dole, Americans reflexively look to government on matters where it has no constitutional or even practical role. The great paradox is that when Americans are asked — in a purely general and philosophical way — if more government involvement is good or bad, they overwhelmingly impart an anti-government view. But when a specific problem arises in the morning affecting their lives, they invariably turn to... government.

Health care is the perfect example of a monstrosity whose problems were caused almost exclusively by government meddling. Pointing to its myriad problems, politicians then claim that only more government intervention can solve them. As Harry Browne says, "The federal government knows how to break your legs, hand you a crutch, and then say, 'If it weren't for government, you wouldn't be able to walk.'"

Republicans pride themselves on having stopped Hillary Clinton's universal takeover of the health care system in the early

'90's and purport to be on the vanguard of its privatization, but by and large the Republicans have acquiesced, or at least accepted the premise that government ought to have a role in health care. President Bush talks more about prescription drugs than does his local pharmacist.

Right now, government spends half of every health care dollar in America — more than insurance companies, employers and individuals. Health care costs are through the roof. Health Maintenance Organizations (HMOs) are now so powerful that politicians are fighting over whose "Patients' Bill of Rights" is more effective in protecting people from HMOs. Of course, it was government that made HMOs so powerful in the first place.

In fact, it is really no mystery how America's health care system, once so efficient and affordable, became such a nightmare. Politicians glory in the current health care mess and have presented themselves as the potential saviors of the system. In reality, the best thing government can do is get out of the health care business altogether. Starting today.

Before the federal government intruded into health care in the 1960's, health insurance was affordable to virtually everyone. Hospital stays did not cost prohibitive amounts, and doctors made house calls. Removing government can restore those days, and with modern technology, health care can once again be efficient, easily accessible and affordable.

How health care arrived at its current state is directly related to original government intrusion. Subsidies pushed up the demand for medical services, while massive regulation placed suppliers out of the market. Moreover, government affects health care costs through the federal income tax code, which allows employers to deduct employee health costs from the employers' taxable income, but does not permit employees or self-employed persons to deduct much of their medical costs. Government has also enacted laws forcing health insurance companies to cover various treatments. And general regulations have been imposed on doctors, hospitals, insurance companies and pharmaceutical manufacturers. All of these actions have caused costs to skyrocket, while doing nothing to improve care.

Government caused all these problems, then steps in to try and save the system it already so thoroughly corrupted. There is indeed a health care crisis in America, but it is a crisis of government. Despite the clear evidence, socialist legislators (Republicans and Democrats) want to blame the free market and create a system in the image of the disastrous European and Canadian models, where care is rationed and people wait five years for heart surgery.

Today, insurance companies have been forced to charge more than most people can afford. Before government intrusion, the poor were not wanting for medical care. There were always doctors and hospitals who could provide low-cost care. Then government invented Medicare (for seniors) and Medicaid (for the poor) and those very people are now disproportionately dependent on those services, which have proven to be bastions of waste and corruption.

When insurance companies were forced to cover every small service, instead of the extraordinary emergencies they were originally intended to cover, the prices ran up for everyone. Just as automobile insurance is not used for oil changes, gasoline and basic repairs, health insurance was not intended to cover every conceivable medical service. By forcing this on companies, government drove up demand. When people realize that everything is covered, they are inclined to take full advantage. This has proven to be a financial catastrophe. Government, after creating this situation, insists on intruding further to make things even worse.

Medicare, Medicaid and HMOs

It is the height of government irresponsibility that so many senior citizens are locked into Medicare. The skyrocketing of medical costs has its genesis with the advent of Medicare and Medicaid in 1965. As even the most novice economic mind can deduce, when all sorts of additional non-emergency services are offered as part of a medical plan, with no out-of-pocket expense for the client, the demand increases, while the supply is limited by regulation. This natural inertia will result in higher prices.

The rules, guidelines and instructions for Medicare are all compiled in a tiny little package of 111,000 pages. And when Congress promises to reform the system and make it easier to understand, to eliminate waste and corruption, and to provide more choice, Americans can bet their hospital gurneys that the true result will be a Medicare system even more complicated.

Medicare has bombarded doctors with regulations, forced them to undercharge and actually driven many out of the medical profession entirely. Some have resigned from the Medicare and Medicaid systems and refused to perform any service paid for by Medicare or Medicaid. By doing this they have been able to reduce their fees by half or more. So Medicare has run up the cost of health care — even for people who are not part of it.

The factual truth that has emerged about Medicare is that it turns down roughly 20 percent of all the care doctors deem necessary. If Medicare denies a claim, it can take a year for the patient's appeal to be processed. If Medicare refuses a particular treatment or medical test, the patient cannot pay the doctor directly for it because if the doctor accepts the money, he would be expelled from Medicare and lose all his other Medicare patients for two years.

Moreover, because Medicare regulations are so cumbersome, ignorance of the law can land a doctor in legal trouble for an honest technical violation. The cruel fact is that senior citizens pay at least twice as much for health care than seniors paid before the creation of Medicare — even after allowing for Medicare's contribution and adjusting for inflation.

The "Medicare + Choice" bill included demands that managed-care providers add more services without being compensated for them. So many providers were facing dreadful losses that over 100 chose to leave the Medicare system entirely, forcing over 100,000 senior citizens to find new plans.

Medicaid is a federally-sponsored program which provides health care to low income people and to nursing homes for the elderly. Though it is run by the states, 50 to 75 percent of the money comes from the federal government. Already, this is a recipe for disaster. In order to make up the difference for what the feds don't provide, states generally raise taxes while upward price pressures generate. The states frequently exceed their budgets. Oregon instituted strict rationing of health care to bring medical costs under control. The Republican governor of Tennessee was forced to break a campaign promise and propose the first income tax in state history, citing out-of-control Medicaid costs as his reasoning.

Before 1965, the poor had access to charity hospitals, free clinics and low prices for health care. Most people think that their own cost in Medicare and Medicaid is limited to what they pay in taxes. But the fact is that doctors, clinics and hospitals must make up for what government won't pay by charging the customers.

In 1973, Congress passed the HMO Act which subsidized HMOs and forced any company providing employee health insurance to offer an HMO as an option. This requirement was repealed in 1995, but the special advantages acquired by HMOs became so entrenched that politicians began offering various "Patients' Bill of Rights" plans to offset the problem they created in the first place.

Depending on the state, insurance companies may be forced to allow for various treatments that the average person will never utilize. This unfairly makes the price of coverage soar. Psychiatric treatment, chiropractors, drug abuse, alcoholism, cosmetic surgery, treatments to stop smoking, treatment for obesity, Christian Science practitioners and many other types of care are forced into policies. There is nothing inherently wrong with any of these treatments. But a person should not have to pay for coverage that they may never use.

Since every medical interest group lobbies politicians tirelessly to force its treatment to be covered by insurers, health insurance becomes more expensive. People in their 20's and 30's cannot afford it and make the choice of risking going without coverage. Then the same politicians who created this predicament bemoan the fact that millions of Americans are going without health coverage. So, they posture, the government must step in. And the cycle repeats itself endlessly.

Government involvement in health care needs desperately to be euthanized — put to sleep forever, never to be heard from again.

Court Tyranny a Liberal Creation

It is nothing less than a delicious irony that liberals, who have depended for so long on undemocratic dictatorial courts to enact their agenda, are the ones bemoaning the actions of the United States Supreme Court (USSC). The current disdain with which liberals hold the USSC is articulated in the nonsensical notion that a "partisan" court "handed" the presidency to George W. Bush. What comes around goes around, indeed.

Liberals have been all over the airwaves accusing conservatives of hypocrisy — pointing out that conservatives claim to believe in "judicial restraint" and "strict constructionism," as well as "states' rights," yet applauded the USSC's intervention in a state matter to give President-elect Bush a victory. Not only is this not simply an oversimplification, it is a total misstatement of what the USSC actually did. In the first place, the USSC did not overturn the laws enacted by the Florida legislature (which is what true activist courts do), it overturned the kangaroo ruling of the Florida Supreme Court (FSC), essentially *striking down* judicial activism, rather than engaging in it. Secondly, the conservative view of appropriate jurisprudence on the part of courts is a deference to the political branches of government — the legislatures and, to a similar degree, the executive. It is those branches which are closest to the people and whose members are most susceptible to the punishment of voters.

It was the FSC which clearly engaged in partisanship by

violating the United States Constitution (changing the rules of an election after the election had taken place) and rewriting a law enacted by the political branch of government — the Florida legislature.

The USSC does indeed have three members regularly identified as "conservative" and two others who are nominally thought of as "conservative," thereby forming the five-vote majority in the presidential ruling. But only intellectual dishonesty could compare these five as simply the inverse of liberal activists. In the judiciary, there is really no such thing as "conservative activist" judges in the same sense that there are "liberal activists." Conservative jurists do not legislate conservative laws from the bench, but merely restrain themselves to interpreting the constitutionality of laws. Liberal jurists are traditionally "result-oriented," meaning they put the cart before the horse. *First*, they arrive at the result they want, and *then* they concoct some tortured justification for their ruling.

A perfect example would be how courts handle a death penalty law. A conservative jurist would merely decide whether such a law was constitutional and leave his own personal views on the death penalty at home. Liberal activist judges who oppose the death penalty would be acting in a perfectly consistent manner by upholding such a law as constitutional, notwithstanding their own opposition to capital punishment. The activist, however, strikes the law down simply because he doesn't like it. This is exactly what happened with the Warren Court, which struck down all capital punishment laws in the fifty states in 1966, although the death penalty is clearly permitted by the United States Constitution.

Similarly, contrary to the conventional wisdom, it is intellectually consistent to both support abortion rights and oppose the USSC's *Roe vs. Wade* decision. While it is difficult to find persons harboring both views in American public life, it is not impossible. Gore attorney and Harvard Professor Laurence Tribe is a constitutional scholar and political liberal who supports abortion rights, but who has derided the *Roe vs. Wade* decision as "terrible law." His point is that the Court acted in an irresponsible (activist) manner by striking down all anti-abortion laws as unconstitutional simply because the Court didn't agree with the laws. There was nothing actually unconstitutional about them. Tribe would simply leave the matter to the states.

This is exactly what is meant by "states' rights" and judicial restraint. Conservatives do not want a Supreme Court ruling that would outlaw abortion (which would be an example of the misnomer "conservative activism"), but merely want *Roe vs. Wade* overturned in order to return the matter to the fifty state legislatures — the political branches of government most answerable to the people. Erroneous political rhetoric aside, a *Roe* reversal would not outlaw abortion, but would force state legislatures to make their own laws on it, in the same way each state has its own death penalty law. Reality is that in the year 2001, there is no state in the Union which would make abortion illegal. But the liberal position is still hysterical vehemence in support of *Roe vs. Wade* because they prefer judicial tyranny — a government of wolves — to the voice of a democratically elected legislature. This is simply how liberals get what they want.

None of the laws which liberals hail as America's greatest achievements were ever enacted by legislatures, but were rather created by court intervention and activism trumping the will of the people. It is an amusing spectacle watching them wail against the United States Supreme Court, an institution liberals once thought of as God.

The Ultimate Price of Quotas

The injustices inflicted by the insidious practice of affirmative action usually relate to the unfair denial of a job, promotion or college entrance to an unqualified or less-qualified minority. The loss can be measured by the barometers of economics, opportunity and plain fairness. In certain instances, however, people have been literally killed by affirmative action.

Proving that not all quotas are created equal, when affirmative action is applied to fire departments, the price to be paid can be death. In 1988, federal judge Marilyn Patel of the California Northern District Court issued a consent decree mandating a fire department made up of 40 percent non-whites and ten percent women. When the San Francisco Fire Department was forced to comply, standards were abandoned and the lives of citizens and firefighters were put dangerously at risk.

Basic tests of strength were replaced with exercises that a child could master. For example, raising a 24 foot ladder to the vertical position requires a high degree of strength and coordination. But because of the new "standards," the base of the ladder is conveniently attached to the ground with a *metal hinge* during the test. Of course, fires are rarely so kind as to start only where there are metal hinges on the sidewalk.

Rather than demonstrate the ability to carry an above-average sized man down a staircase, the new "test" merely requires an applicant to *drag* a 40 pound cloth dummy across a *polished* cement floor and out the door. If only the typical person in a burning building weighed 40 pounds and could be dragged instead of carried, and if fires were considerate enough to ignite in one-story buildings only.

In the early 1990's when the first Hispanic female firefighter — an affirmative action hire — was assigned in San Francisco, the news was greeted with elaborate fanfare. In fact, a local Spanish television station went so far as to film her during her mandatory daily drills. After she repeatedly dropped the most light-weight ladder on her head, the station politely left without filing the story. Eventually, her supervisor offered to design a weight training program for her, so she could improve her strength. In response, she filed a complaint with the Equal Employment Opportunity Commission against the supervisor for suggesting she lacked strength.

According to Ray Batz, now retired after 30 years in the Department, a quota female firefighter, after having climbed a 50-foot ladder onto a roof, announced that she felt "dehydrated," and promptly climbed down to get a drink of water.

"Another woman," Batz recalled, "told to connect a hose to a water source while her crew advanced the nozzle 100 feet closer to the seat of the fire, simply left the building without giving them water. 'It was too hot,'" Batz remembers her saying.

Batz also recalls working alongside an affirmative action female hire who could not break a sheetrock wall with her standard 8-pound ax. Her lieutenant became so aggravated that he broke the wall with the *back of his hand*.

But the comical yet tragic anecdotes of affirmative action in the fire department are not only the province of the physical tests. Because non-whites could not pass the basic intelligence test that the Department historically required, the written exam had to be dumbed down. One question on the exam now asks the stumper, "Which is more difficult, pushing a wheelbarrow up a ramp or on the flat?"

Duh.

After San Francisco hired an outside testing company at a cost of $250,000 to design the promotional exam for the rank of lieutenant, every ethnic and racial firefighters union was asked to evaluate the new exam for that elusive "test bias." All agreed that the test contained no bias. But when only 12 percent of the black applicants passed the test, the Black Firefighters' Association changed it mind, stating that the test was biased *only against blacks*.

Eventually, one black "lieutenant" ordered his crew to respond to an alarm in a parking lot and look for a "Cadillac." The computer print-out in his hand plainly said the victim was a "cardiac," a heart attack victim.

Another affirmative action black lieutenant was hired and promoted way beyond his abilities. Because he did not recognize the signs of an impending "backdraft" (explosion), he remained standing when eight other firefighters knew enough to throw themselves to the floor. In this case, affirmative action killed the man.

Regrettably, fires don't possess the manners to break out only where these laws of lunacy are not practiced. When former New York City Mayor Ed Koch was asked about ethnic diversity in his fire department, he said he was more interested in whether a firefighter could carry a 200 pound mayor out of a burning building.

Wackos at Waco Finally Confess

For six and a half years the FBI has denied in the most strident terms having done anything that could possibly have started the inferno that killed over 80 people — including many children — at the Davidian compound in Waco, Texas. For six and a half years they have lied.

Attorney General Janet Reno, who claims to be shocked and angered by last week's revelation that the FBI did indeed unleash pyrotechnic devices into the compound, either honestly did not know — which makes her incompetent — or was herself complicit in one of the most criminal government cover-ups in United States history.

This truth has come forward now for two reasons. First, the civil lawsuit brought by victims' family members will soon be commencing and the evidence compiled by honest Texas Rangers will reveal the FBI's sinister role. Secondly, the government felt it would simply be easier to put its own spin on the revelation if it came forward unilaterally. Already, the FBI is claiming, yes, we did use flashbangs despite the fact that we've denied it for six and a half years; but, we used them hours before the fires started, so they could not possibly have caused the conflagration. Right.

Most military and law-enforcement special operations experts have faulted the BATF (Bureau of Alcohol, Tobacco and Firearms) for a plan tactically and logistically flawed from start to finish. This should come as no surprise to anyone. The only thing that BATF agents ever really do is arrest petrified, non-violent gun dealers who have violated gun control laws, and raid firecracker storage warehouses to confiscate illegal fireworks. Neither activity is risky, and none of it prepares agents for the kind of raid that even the Israeli Mossad would feel nervous about.

The BATF claims that it suffered heavy casualties because of strict "rules of engagement" that do not permit shooting without a definite target. This is a lie, and is clearly contradicted by broadcast video showing agents exercising very poor fire control, firing blindly with automatic weapons over vehicles with little or no sight picture.

Frank Bolz, Jr., a former hostage negotiator with 28 years experience in the New York City Police Department, said, "Once you know you have children in there, you don't go storming in." The former Waco District Attorney, Vic Feazell, condemned the BATF's "storm trooper tactics" as "a vulgar display of power on the part of the feds."

Allegations surfaced as far back as 1993 from sources inside the BATF, that BATF commanders lied to Texas Governor Ann Richards. Apparently, agents told Richards that they needed use of a National Guard helicopter for use in a "drug" investigation — the only legal basis upon which the helicopter could be loaned to BATF. In truth, there was never even a suspicion of drug involvement by the Branch Davidians. The allegations of drug use by the cult, which were further fostered in an effort to quiet Texas officials who suspected a BATF lie, were denounced by a BATF source as "made up ... out of whole cloth ... a complete fabrication."

And inside sources have revealed that BATF leaders lied to their own men, failing to tell them that the helicopter had taken fire from the compound before the ground assault actually began. This means that BATF ground teams went into the compound without even knowing that some of their own men had been fired upon. Their leaders had this knowledge, but said nothing.

Claims by BATF that they were concerned with the safety of compound occupants, so much so that BATF agents took heavy casualties themselves, has also been shown to be a lie. In addition to firing upon the Branch Davidians without provocation, and the wild, unaimed and purposeless firing of automatic weapons, it is now widely believed that federal shooters were armed with special armor piercing ammunition. With such ammo in hand, what concern for the safety of occupants did BATF have in mind?

As to the basis for the initial raid, it is now becoming clear that the BATF had absolutely no good evidence to support a warrant for a search of the compound. Review of the warrant issued by U.S. Magistrate Judge Dennis G. Green discloses that there was not one single piece of hard evidence against the Branch Davidians which would lawfully support a warrant. The BATF claims to have been searching for machine guns, yet no one quoted in the affidavit which accompanies the warrant could state definitively that any compound occupant owned a machine gun. And to this day, it appears that not one automatic weapon has been recovered from the ruins at Waco. Also, claims of "child abuse" by David Koresh were a joke, not only because they were previously investigated by Texas officials and not pursued, but because the BATF has no authority or jurisdiction of any kind over child welfare matters.

After the disastrous February raid, control over the Waco matter was handed over to the FBI, which proceeded onward with the murder of the Branch Davidians. The list of FBI lies used to justify the April 19, 1993 raid is endless.

First, the FBI claims it tried to bring the matter to a peaceful end. Untrue. The FBI heightened tensions with its "Tokyo Rose" psychological tactics and unwillingness to listen to experts who opined that a violent end was imminent if force was used against the Branch Davidians again.

The FBI claims that it used tear gas in an effort to remove occupants from the compound without death. This is a blatant lie. The tear gas used by the FBI is so dangerous that its use has been banned in international warfare. Also, its use indoors is not recommended, as an overdose can easily occur which can lead to death.

The FBI similarly claims that it pumped the gas into one part of the building so that the occupants would escape out the other end of the structure. But if this is so, why did the military vehicle used to smash the walls of the Branch Davidian home destroy stairways which lead to the other end of the structure, trapping occupants in one portion of the gas-impregnated building and making such escape impossible?

The FBI claims that the danger from fire was minimal, but every credible expert strongly disagreed. The smashing of the building and electrical wiring, coupled with the threat of gunfire and a hot, dry atmosphere, created an intolerable risk of fire.

But the biggest explosion may yet blow the lid off this obscene cover-up. The perpetrators deserve what is coming to them.

What Ashcroft Faced in Missouri

John Ashcroft has finally been confirmed as United States Attorney General, and the faint howls of hysterical liberals can still be heard. One is reminded of Dracula's ear-shattering screams turned to mild simpering as Van Helsing drove the stake deeper into his heart. Not since the confirmation of Clarence Thomas to the Supreme Court have liberals galvanized their oddball troops to derail such a superbly qualified conservative.

At the height of the confirmation drama, the standard charges of "racism" and "insensitivity" were hurled at Ashcroft, with the primary focus on then-Senator Ashcroft's crusade to prevent black jurist Ronnie White from being elevated to the federal bench. Ashcroft's opposition to White, of course, had absolutely nothing to do with race and everything to do with White's controversial opinion on a death penalty matter.

Other instances of Ashcroft's right-wing sins committed as governor, attorney general and U.S. Senator from Missouri were also mentioned by liberals and the media, some in more detail than others. It was vaguely touched upon that Ashcroft had "opposed" the "desegregation" fight in the Kansas City school system. The details of this particular catastrophe were merely glossed over. Had Americans actually heard exactly what Ashcroft opposed, the Senate switchboard would have crashed due to a million calls of support for him.

The effort to racially integrate the Kansas City public schools will be recorded as perhaps the most outrageous example of social engineering in the history of the United States. In the name of racial equality, a dictator federal judge single-handedly raised taxes without any input from the Missouri legislature, raided the treasuries of both Kansas City and the state of Missouri, and created gold-plated schools that would in theory lure whites out of the suburbs.

The Kansas City school system began in September 1867 with five schools -- four for whites and one for blacks. By law, the schools were segregated; but also by law, black schools were to be equal to the white ones. Black teachers were paid the same salaries as whites and the same amount was spent on students of both races. In 1936-37, it cost $79.31 to educate a white student, and $69.10 for a black child. Nevertheless, blacks were sometimes slighted in capital budgets, so in 1949 parents at the all-black Bruce elementary school sued the city to repair their school. The Missouri courts denied the suit on the grounds that white schools were no better off. History now records that all students received excellent education in Kansas City's segregated schools.

After the *Brown v. Board Education* ruling in 1954, desegregation commenced. Students were then required to simply attend the schools nearest their homes, regardless of race. But like everywhere else in the country, the schools remained largely segregated because of voluntarily segregated housing patterns. Whites lived in white neighborhoods and blacks in black neighborhoods. The small number of white students who were zoned for black schools simply moved away. The schools were no more integrated than before because white parents did not want their children in black schools.

By the 1970's, whites from Kansas City did what whites all over America did -- engage in "white flight" to the suburbs to escape the increasing number of blacks in the city. By the mid-'70's, two-thirds of the Kansas City students were black. Naturally, what followed was the usual crime, disintegration of school buildings and rapidly declining test scores. In 1977, the Kansas City school board sued to force 18 white suburban school districts into one single huge district, to both get the white suburbs' tax money for the crumbling district and to force busing on white students.

In 1985, Judge Russell Clark embarked on a tyrannical integration plan. He rationalized that only stellar, million-dollar schools could lure bigoted whites out of the suburbs, which he further assumed would rejuvenate the schools and raise black test scores. His premise was so misguided that it should have been killed in the womb. His actions so tyrannical he should have been impeached.

In ten years, Judge Clark spent more than $1.4 billion. He spent $418 million on new construction. He ordered a school demolished and a brand new one built in its place -- from a rare limestone in order to make the school an architectural landmark. Scores of houses were ordered bulldozed to make room. The judge ordered planetariums, Olympic-size swimming pools with underwater observation windows, dust-free diesel mechanic rooms, a mock-United Nations room wired for simultaneous interpretation, television and radio studios, video editing and animation labs, a courtroom with jury and judge chambers, a model Greek village in which to teach democracy, and one computer for every two children. The former coach of the Soviet Olympic fencing team was even hired to teach his craft.

To pay for this orgy of spending, Judge Clark unilaterally raised Kansas City property taxes, not once but twice -- the first time in American history that a federal judge levied taxes. Judge Clark tried to impose a surcharge on income taxes, but was restrained by an appeals court. After bleeding Kansas City to death, he went after state funds, on the reasoning that Missouri had contributed to segregation by allowing restrictive covenants and by "not doing enough" to promote integration. $800 million was extracted from Missourians outside Kansas City.

In his final act of judicial madness, Judge Clark decreed that he would continue to run the public schools until black scores were as high as whites. This, of course, never happened and could never happen. At the end of Judge Clark's reign of terror, nothing at all changed. The dropout rate of blacks climbed and the attendance rate dropped. The achievement gap between the races remained the same. Test scores were unmoved. And no amount of money could tempt whites out of the suburbs so that their children could sit next to blacks. Yes, this is what John Ashcroft and many other Missourians opposed.

Judge Clark was finally reined in by a 5-4 Supreme Court

decision in 1995, but not before an unprecedented disaster brought on by liberal racial zeal.

The Only Legal Ponzi Scheme

In 1920, an Italian immigrant in Boston named Charles Ponzi devised what he thought to be a brilliant business proposition for himself. He lured investors into his plan by promising to pay them a 50 percent profit on their investment in just 45 days. Quite an appealing rate of return. So appealing, in fact, that scores of suckers poured money into Ponzi's coffers.

In reality, however, Ponzi could not possibly deliver on his promise because the rate of return he guaranteed was simply unattainable. So when an investor wanted to withdraw his principal and interest, Ponzi paid him not with the actual profits made from his initial investment, but with the money he solicited from yet new investors. In such a scheme, therefore, the only way to pay people what they are promised is to contrive a pyramid whereby new money is made off the backs of new investors. The initial investment, of course, never actually makes any money.

Eventually, as common sense dictates, the scheme collapses when demands for repayment cannot be met. Charles Ponzi ended up in jail. And today, the framework of his plan is recognized by law and bears his name -- a "Ponzi scheme" or "pyramid." Anyone who tries this will also be arrested and wind up in jail.

There is one Ponzi scheme, however, that is not only legal but is the object of more political pandering than any other issue in contemporary America. It is called Social Security.

Hatched in 1935, this particular Ponzi scheme is still going. Libertarian presidential candidate Harry Browne succinctly points out the only two differences between Social Security and any other Ponzi scheme. "The politicians won't arrest themselves..." and "The politicians can change the rules whenever necessary to keep the scheme going."

The similarities are more numerous. The original Social Security "trust fund" (what a misnomer) was established on the premise of extorting a portion of taxpayers' money, to be invested by government, and then returned with interest upon retirement. But it was just as impossible for politicians then as now to keep their hands off a large sum of money. So only four years later, in 1939, the rules were changed for the first time.

Taking their cue from Charles Ponzi, the government transformed Social Security into a "pay as you go" system -- a farce in which benefits are paid not from the initial money placed into the fund, but by the taxes paid from current workers. That's why it is so much nonsense hearing seniors say they are only collecting what they "put into it." What seniors put into Social Security is long gone. Social Security is, therefore, not an annuity or retirement fund, but a pyramid sanctioned by law. Unfortunately, the legitimacy of law cannot square the inherent instability of such a scheme, which is why the rules are constantly changed and why politicians incessantly speak of "saving" Social Security. Private employers never speak of "saving" their firm's private pension or annuity plans, because private plans are real and the money placed in them is really there.

Today's young workers who pay the 15 percent Social Security tax every week for their "retirement" are not having their money invested or saved for them. The money goes directly to today's Social Security recipients. It is no wonder that better than two-thirds of today's young workers tell surveys that they do not expect to receive a dime from Social Security when they retire.

By its very nature, Social Security can never be an effective system. It is primarily a *political* program run by politicians for their own political expediency. Like everything else the federal government touches, Social Security is a time-bomb waiting to explode. If it were inherently sound, it wouldn't have to be tinkered with. Even the Bush proposal of allowing a two percent portion to be invested privately by the taxpayer is a joke. The only stable plan is a totally private, voluntary annuity. Not down the road or by some phase-in plan, but right now.

One of the theories behind Social Security is that government must care for people's retirement because some people are just too irresponsible to do it for themselves. It is entirely consistent with the Nanny Government mentality that because some people might be irresponsible, then everyone else must pay for it and suffer. Not only is this tyrannical toward responsible Americans, but assumes that government can handle things best. This is a view at total odds with reality.

Furthermore, as a practical matter, Social Security is a fraudulent rip-off. Unlike private pensions or annuities, Social Security provides only a starvation monthly amount, and absolutely no estate to leave one's descendants. Even a conservative bank savings account would provide a monthly income several times the worth of Social Security and an estate worth hundreds of thousands of dollars.

Because so many Americans are suckers, they actually support *saving* this scheme which is taking them to the cleaners. Beginning today, American workers should withhold the 15 percent Social Security tax and invest it in a private plan offered by insurance companies, which will certainly provide a comfortable retirement and a substantial estate. Today's retirement recipients should have an annuity immediately purchased for them by the government by selling off the trillions of dollars of unnecessary assets the government now holds.

Government should finally be out of the retirement business, not to mention the nanny business altogether. Only in private hands can there be true "social security."

Who Wants to Be a Black Man?

Census workers for the year 2000 will likely experience some head spinning next year when they attempt to decipher the different racial categories which Americans have the option of checking off on census forms. The painstaking task of counting and classifying Americans will increase considerably for government staff as they prepare for the racial madness that awaits them.

Since 1977, the United States government has officially recognized only four races for the purpose of tabulating the census: white, black, Asian-and Pacific-Islander, and American-Indian-and-Eskimo. It also recognizes one ethnicity, Hispanic, and then apportions all Hispanics among the four recognized races. Hybrids (people of mixed race) had to choose one of the four. The government's instructions to these people was "the category which most closely reflects the individual's recognition in his community should be used for purposes of reporting on persons who are of mixed racial and/or ethnic origins." So if your "community" thinks you are black, that's what you are. Although this simplifies things from a mathematical standpoint, it can cause mass confusion in people's minds, as well as statistical inaccuracy.

In an attempt to alleviate some of the rigidity of the racial choices for the 1990 census, the government added the category "other." Four percent of the American people checked "other" and were then divided up by the census bureau into the four racial categories. Many activists were still not satisfied, since "other" fails to distinguish between, say, Arabs and Iranians, and they all ultimately still were placed into one of the four original racial classifications.

In response to all of this, a fifth racial category was proposed in 1997 by activists who wanted the option of choosing "multiracial" for the 2000 census. It became a controversy which pitted one left-wing group (blacks) against another. Thus the incendiary debate began about how black is black, who is black, who wants to be black, and the ramifications of these distinctions gaining official recognition.

The history of racial identification in America is a colorful one (both literally and figuratively). For most of American history, miscegenation (mixed interbreeding) was frowned upon. As recently as 1967, 16 states still had anti-miscegenation laws on the books, before they were struck down by the Supreme Court in *Loving v. Virginia.*

Historically, the United States has followed the "one drop rule," whereby anyone with even a trace of black blood was considered black. This was not only popular thinking, but was also codified in law and census categories. The genesis of the "one drop rule" was in the notion that to possess any black blood was to somehow be tainted, so it would only be appropriate to be considered part of the enslaved race. Therefore, it is ironic that, to a remarkable degree, adherence to the "one drop rule" still exists today, notwithstanding that race-mixing is more socially acceptable. Virtually all American blacks have white blood, yet are still considered — and consider themselves — black. A white candidate for office referred to her two children as "African-American" even though they are actually mulatto. (In fact, since American blacks are of roughly 25 percent European extraction, her children are in reality more white than black.) But the United States, unlike Brazil, has never recognized mulattos or octoroons (persons who are one-eighth black) or any other arcane black-mixed possibility as anything other than black.

Although adding this "multiracial" category to the list may seem chic and progressive, and may actually provide for more accurate classifications, it is blacks — to the everlasting embarrassment of liberals — who most vehemently oppose it and are most jealous in guarding the "one drop rule." Indeed, what was once an implacably hostile method of whites to distance themselves from even the lightest-skinned blacks is now conventional black thinking. Why?

Prof. Jon Michael Spencer of the University of Richmond argues in his book, *The New Colored People*, that there is strength in numbers and he opposes losing any "blacks" to a different racial category. Congressional districts are sometimes drawn to give blacks a majority, and discrimination cases often turn on the number of blacks in a given neighborhood. He also believes the multiracial category will undermine black solidarity, stating that the "multiracial" movement's "real aim is to dismantle the black community."

Spencer quotes another black as arguing "the suggestion today that the one-drop rule is an arbitrary social construction that could be changed sounds to the black community like a dangerous idea. If one result in such a change would be to cause some lighter-colored persons to leave the black community for the white community, the former would lose some of its hard-won political strength, perhaps some of its best leaders..."

Indeed, there is already a mistrust by blacks of their lighter-skinned brethren, according to Prof. Spencer, and he fears an emerging class of "house niggers" who will "kick their darker kindred around even more severely than the whites" and will help whites "to guard their systems of power and privilege." Prof. Spencer also shudders at the thought of white parents telling their hybrid children that Colin Powell, Lena Horne and Alex Haley are "multiracial, just like you."

Promoting the multiracial view are a cadre of whites and mulattos who dislike the "other" category as demeaning. James Landrith, a white man with a black wife, is editor of *The Multiracial Activist*. He complains of "traditional civil rights groups who tend to brush off our community or denigrate us... [and] are the ones battering self-identifying multiracials as 'running from their blackness' and calling them 'Uncle Tom' as well as belittling and demeaning interracial marriage."

Organizations like Project RACE (Reclassify All Children Equally), American Association for Multi-Ethnic Americans, A Place For US, and magazines like *Interrace* are also proponents of the "multiracial" category. And some mulattos and hybrids dislike being told they must be black. Jan Wright writes in *Interracial Voice*, "If you are mixed race, you are often called upon to prove your Blackness, as though a lack of melanin proves that you don't want to 'uplift the race.'" She desires not to be half black, but "Black AND White."

Nevertheless, Prof. Spencer's contention is buttressed by other mulattos quoted in his book, one of whom rejects his whiteness, stating, "Until the last remnant of white racism is verifiably eliminated from the Earth, all 'non-whites' -- however one defines that -

- must contribute to the continuation and the strengthening of the ... 'fundamental racial distinction' in America by identifying solely with their/our non-European roots."

The prevalence of this view is ostensibly proven by the government study of the "multiracial" category proposal. In a survey, only one percent of blacks chose the multiracial category, and even fewer whites did.

Now the verdict is in and the Office of Management and Budget (OMB), which makes the decision for the Census Bureau, has concluded that the multiracial category would "create another population group, and no doubt add to racial tension and further fragmentation of our population." Instead, hybrids may check as many of the four original racial categories as they wish, which will undoubtedly create mass confusion and lots of headaches for next year's census workers.

Ah, the wonders of diversity.

# IV

CRIME AND GUN CONTROL

Finally: The Truth About Race and Hate Crimes

A new study which exposes the truth about racial crime rates, hate crimes and interracial violence is so stunning in its revelations and so profound in its implications, that it may finally blow the lid off the myths that have shrouded reality for so long. The findings released by the New Century Foundation in a study entitled, "The Color of Crime," announced during a nationally-televised press conference on C-Span, are so earth-shattering that even liberal stalwarts such as Senators Edward Kennedy and Russell Feingold, as well as Republican Senator John McCain, have requested copies of the report. Copies have also been requested by the National Association of Police Organizations and the New Jersey State Police (which came under fire for "racial profiling.")

While Americans are inundated and overwhelmed with reports of hate crimes committed by whites — invariably accompanied by front-page news and national breast-beating — the true facts can only be described as shocking. The numbers revealed are derived from the U.S. Department of Justice's National Victimization Survey (NCVS), Hate Crime Statistics provided by the FBI, and other local and national law enforcement records put together by the FBI and the Department of Justice.

The findings are so startling that two strategies are likely to emerge from those who simply will not like the results. The first will be to ignore the data and continue to wail about white wickedness. The second will be to deny the facts with political double-talk. In any event, those who wish to discredit the study will find themselves in the awkward position of claiming that the New Century Foundation is in cahoots with the United States government.

Contrary to what people may realize, there is a difference between interracial crime and what the government identifies as a "hate crime." Interracial crimes are those in which perpetrators of one race victimize people of another race. The motive of bias is not necessarily known unless the perpetrators use racial slurs. "Hate crimes" are those in which it is determined that bias was the motive behind the crime.

Incredibly, there is an enormous disparity between interracial crimes and hate crimes. Although hate crimes receive the most attention, the most recent data show that there were approximately 1.7 million instances of interracial crime, compared to only 9,861 "hate crimes." It is unrealistic, to say the least, that of the 1.7 million figure for interracial crimes, none were motivated by bias. But even taking these figures at face value, *90 percent of interracial violence is committed by blacks against whites.* Blacks are, therefore, up to *250 times* more likely to commit acts of violence against whites than the reverse. And even with the low number of hate crimes which the government acknowledges, blacks are still twice as likely as whites to commit them. Clearly, all of this goes against the popular perception of interracial and hate crimes being the province of white perpetrators and non-white victims.

The report also finds that there is more black-on-white crime than black-on-black crime, again putting the lie to the popular notion that most black crime is committed against other blacks. When blacks commit crimes of violence, they choose white victims 56.3 percent of the time. Conversely, when whites commit violence, they choose blacks as victims only 2.6 percent of the time. It would seem to be impossible to discover numbers that are more at odds with the public perception regarding interracial crimes of violence.

An interesting ancillary but significant note to the findings is that to the extent that the numbers are skewed, they are skewed against whites. In the official "Hate Crime Incident Report" which is filled out by police after every bias incident, Hispanics are listed in the victim category, *but not in the perpetrator category.* So, as the study points out, "A Mexican who is attacked because of ethnicity is recorded as Hispanic, but if the same Mexican attacks a black or white for racial reasons he is considered white. This inflates the figures for 'white' hate crime perpetrators, and gives the impression that Hispanics commit no hate crimes." This has also given rise to the ridiculous statistic of hate crimes committed by whites against whites (!) which are obviously committed by Hispanics.

In pure crime rates (against any race), blacks commit violent crimes at four to nine times the white rate. Hispanics commit violence at approximately three times the white race. Asians commit these crimes at only one-half to three-quarters the white rate.

The stark numbers of black crime are so enormous that the study points out that blacks are as much more dangerous than whites as men are more dangerous than women. From a statistical and common sense point of view, people are justified in being more fearful of a group of unknown men than of a group of unknown women. Using the same standard, therefore, it is just as reasonable to distinguish between black men and white men when taking precautions.

What this means, according to New Century Foundation President Jared Taylor, is that, "This is the painful reality that gives rise to 'racial profiling.' Police quickly learn who the bad guys are. When there is a murder they don't look for little old ladies. They look for young men—unfortunately, they are often justified in looking for young black men."

What the New Century Foundation has done is simply take information that is readily available to anyone, but which has irresponsibly been ignored by major media and legislators — until now. Let some honest discussion lead, finally, to some honest solutions.

To order "The Color of Crime," visit the New Century website, amren.com.

Race, Crime and Guns

One of the more ludicrous arguments that gun control advocates use to justify their madness is the notion that there is less violent crime in countries that have tight gun prohibitionist laws than in the

United States, which, by comparison, allows for wide availability of firearms.

It is quite true that when compared to certain European nations, America does indeed suffer from a discernibly higher crime scourge. The murder rate in the U.S. is roughly 9.3 per 100,000 citizens. It is 7.4 in Britain; 6.0 in Italy; 4.6 in France; and 4.2 in Germany. All of these European countries essentially deny by law the right of citizens the private ownership of firearms. A comparison to gun-free Japan would show similar results.

What is crucial to understand, however, is that gun controllers have always been, and continue to be, shameless liars. Their argument is Hobbesian at best, and deliberately excludes all other factors. On its face, their vacuous position correlates one fact with another and infers that the same fact *causes* the other. For example, no football team that plays in a domed stadium has ever been to the Super Bowl. One could conclude, therefore, that playing in domes is simply not conducive to winning enough games to get to the Super Bowl. The reality is, upon even a cursory inspection, that great teams have simply never been those who happen to play in domes.

But even this rebuttal assumes the gun controllers' basic facts to be correct. They are not. In Switzerland, every man of military age keeps a fully automatic rifle in his home. The Swiss have a minuscule murder rate. Likewise in Israel, the population is heavily armed, but Israelis rarely shoot each other.

The further implication is that American culture is somehow impacted by a "wild west" mentality that gives rise to a unique amount of violence. Setting aside the fact that every reliable study for thirty years demonstrates that crime is *higher* in American locales with tight gun control than in cities with right to carry laws, the most crucial factor in analyzing crime numbers is totally ignored by those who trumpet the fraudulent gun control argument.

That crucial factor is, of course, race.

It is disingenuous, to say the least, to compare America's crime rate with other nations' while ignoring the differing murder and robbery rates of America's different races. The murder rate for blacks is 43 per 100,000; for whites it is 5.1 per 100,000 — only one-eighth the black rate. The robbery rate for blacks is 1,343 per 100,000 — ten times the white rate. What this means is that the murder rate for American whites is *lower* than that of Britain or Italy, *despite the fact that American whites have wide access to guns and Brits and Italians do not.*

So the presence of blacks alone — with no other factor needed to consider — has pushed American crime rates higher than those of European countries. Furthermore, the "white" crime rates are artificially high, since Hispanics are counted as "white" when the government tabulates criminal perpetrators (Hispanics suddenly stop being white when the government counts *victims* of crime.) Americans, of course, will look long and hard for any politician with the testosterone to point this out, no matter how obvious it may be.

Ignoring race is not merely political expedience to be laughed off. There are serious policy implications. Whites are impacted profoundly by gun control laws that are enacted because of the crimes committed by blacks. Now, no one would seriously entertain the prospect of separate laws for the separate races, but race is certainly considered when it suits the needs of the extreme liberal agenda.

Affirmative action, for example, is based on the premise (however misguided) that racial quotas are needed to compensate for white racism. There are indeed two sets of racial rules. Blacks get the job or the promotion based on race — and no other consideration — because the "playing field" is somehow tilted in the favor of whites. Bear in mind that this standard is applied across the board, without any one individual proof of a specific wrong inflicted on a given black, or a specific act of malice by a given white.

Would the geniuses who thought this up apply the same standard to criminal justice? If whites are more likely to be racist and blacks more likely to be the victims of it, and these facts justify affirmative action, then what about the availability of guns? Should stricter sentencing laws, as well as gun laws, be applied to blacks since they are so overwhelmingly more likely to commit violent crimes?

If the pointy-headed bureaucrats who invented discrimination and injustice against whites — affirmative action — ever applied their standard with a semblance of consistency, they would indeed find themselves advocating for such laws. But hypocrisy, not consistency, has always been their true standard.

Abortion, Crime and Race

A shocking new study that links the extraordinarily high rate of abortion in the United States with the national drop in crime has the two most disparate groups in America agreeing with each other. Fanatical pro-lifers despise the finding, while pro-choicers seem to be ignoring it.

Interestingly, while the study appears to show a convincing correlation between abortion and less crime — a fact that would bolster the pro-choice cause — it is pro-choicers and major media that seem most intent on dismissing the story. Why? Probably because of the racial angle.

The study, conducted by Steven Levitt of the University of Chicago and John Donohue III, a law professor at Stanford University, concludes that the decrease in crime since 1991 is at least half attributable to the legalization of abortion through the *Roe v. Wade* Supreme Court decision in 1973. It seems that the timing of these events is crucial to the validity of the study. Crime is overwhelmingly the province of men between the ages of 18 and 24. The theory, therefore, is that so many potential criminals — who would have reached their peak crime-prone years in 1991 — were simply never born.

This is a startling argument. Certainly, the researchers deserve credit for having the courage to bring their findings forward. The single greatest indicator of crime rate in a given locale is race. It is a fact that nonwhites proportionately commit the most crimes. But the second greatest indicator is the age of a population. There are roughly one million abortions per year in the United States, a horrific number under any circumstances, but even more profound given that there are also 4.1 million births. This means that one in four pregnancies ends in abortion. Blacks and other minorities have 40 percent of abortions, a figure that is almost double the minority percentage in the general population.

So Levitt and Donohue are arguing that a less criminal-minded group of teenagers was born and came of age beginning in 1991 than otherwise would have been without all those nonwhite abortions. Clearly, the racial aspect of this cannot be overlooked. Between 1991 and 1997, the murder rate has fallen 31 percent; the violent crime rate has fallen 19 percent and the property crime rate 16 percent. So what has the fallout of this study actually been?

The story was broken by the *Chicago Tribune*, which gave it front page coverage. The *New York Times* relegated the story to page A-14 and the *Washington Post* ran it on page A-9. A Nexus search reveals that only one opinion piece has been written on the study, that by economist Robert J. Samuelson in *Newsweek*. In a thoughtful essay entitled, "Do We Care About Truth?" Samuelson attempts to uncover why such an earth-shattering study has been largely ignored. While he only touches on the racial aspect of the report, Samuelson does strike at the heart of the issue with his subtitle, "But people ignore what they find upsetting."

While conceding that the researchers' evidence is largely circumstantial, Samuelson is rightly disturbed that a free press in a free society refuses to tackle it head on. He writes, "There's a temptation to embrace self-censorship: let's drop the issue... our understanding of crime will suffer if we can't debate one plausible cause of its decline."

Samuelson is obviously correct. Ideological rigidity and fanaticism are the most all too common reasons why people ignore facts they find unpleasant or which refute their alleged beliefs. One pro-life group calls the study, "fraught with stupidity." Such a reaction is especially distressing coming from pro-lifers, a group generally comprised of persons of the right. This type of intellectual dishonesty and cowardice is usually the realm of liberals, especially on matters of race. A more responsible position, at the very least, would be to deplore abortion on moral grounds while allowing for the possibility that the study has factual merit — on the order of supporting the death penalty as a matter of justice, while acknowledging that it might not be a deterrent. To dismiss the study out of hand without fair examination is irresponsible.

It is important to understand that the researchers' motives are not to promote abortion. They are criminologists who simply could not ignore the stark numbers. Levitt and Donohue also point out that the decrease in crime is also attributable to longer prison sentences. In fact, they show that the premature release of just one prisoner results in 15 more crimes the following year. Clearly a case in support of more jail space.

As for the pro-choice take on the study, there doesn't appear to be much of one, except for the deafening silence. Normally, pro-choicers jump at the opportunity to exploit statistics in their favor, whatever those may be. But it would certainly prove to be one of the all-time great awkward moments in broadcast history, watching the Clintons and Planned Parenthood publicly applaud a finding which shows abortion as an anti-crime measure. The incestuous battle between minority activists and other pro-choicers would be a spectacle to behold.

The Million Nut March

John O'Sullivan, the British-born editor of the conservative *National Review* magazine in the early 1990's, put forward a doctrine which he christened "O'Sullivan's Law." The tenet of "O'Sullivan's Law" was that any foundation — any organization funded through grants which ostensibly functioned as part-activist, part-think tank — *which was not overtly right-wing*, would inevitably become left-wing.

O'Sullivan's point was that even foundations that were not originally conceived as left-wing, but rather were neutral in ideological impetus, would by natural inertia become left-wing because liberal activists are naturally drawn to that which spends other people's money. Furthermore, O'Sullivan asserted, as long as a foundation did not espouse a specific right-wing cause, that given organization was more easily co-opted by liberals. Therefore, an ideologically benign foundation designed simply to "promote literacy" or further "cultural awareness" would eventually fall into the hands of the left. "O'Sullivan's Law" has proven to be true in much more than foundations.

Something called the "Million Mom March," which has burst onto the national scene, purports to be a grassroots galvanization of "concerned mothers" across America who will be marching on Washington, D.C. on Mother's Day in response to the media-hyped school shootings in the past year. It is politically treacherous grounds to be seen to be criticizing "mom and apple pie," especially when the cause they're marching for seems so sensible and agreeable. But the name itself, derived from Louis Farrakhan's "Million Man March," is an indicator of the politics of this laughable display of hysterical left-wing activism. At least Farrakhan was honest about his intentions.

The "Million Mom March" cloaks its zaniness in some soft language, but the hard left component of its core is ever so slightly beneath the surface. As "O'Sullivan's Law" points out, the "Million Mom March," even if it was not originally conceived by the left — and there is ample enough evidence that it was — has fallen into its decrepit hands.

Organizers of the March state that its purpose is "dedicated to the mission of educating our children and our country about the life-threatening danger of guns." How original. Until now, no one knew that guns were potentially life-threatening. So do the mothers want better safety training and responsible instruction for children? Not on your life. What do they want? More gun control, of course. Now that's *really* original.

The agenda of the "Million Mom March" reads like a laundry list of some of the nuttiest and irresponsible ideas — pulled out of the microwave — that have come down the Washington Beltway. These tired demands have already so miserably failed everywhere they've been tried that it's remarkable that the March has gotten the attention it has. But that is probably *why* it has gotten the attention. Liberals never recognize their own failures.

The Marchers want to trash the Second Amendment and the right to bear arms. Let's stop these killings by cracking down on the law-abiding citizens! Nowhere do the mothers demand the death penalty, an end to parole, a limit to procedural extensions of criminals' rights, armed guards in schools, rights of principals to expel hoodlum students or any serious anti-crime measure. Only gun control.

They want "cooling off periods and extensive background checks" for gun purchasers. (Never mind that all the perpetrators in these school shootings were or would have been totally unaffected by such nonsensical laws.) They also want "licensing and registration" of all handguns. (Here comes confiscation.) And "safety locks" for all handguns. (The new pet panacea of hysterical gun controllers.) They also want "no-nonsense enforcement of existing gun laws." (In other words, keep trying to enforce the 20,000-plus gun control laws that still haven't stopped crime. Presumably this demand is intended to counter "*nonsense* enforcement of existing gun laws.") The Marchers round out their demands with the tried-and-true "one handgun per month" limit on purchases which hardened criminals are sure to obey.

The organizers are trying to recruit "honorary mothers" for this farce, support the ridiculous "guns for sneakers" programs that have become commonplace and vow to patronize "nonviolent sponsors" who attach their names to the march.

And just who is endorsing the "Million Mom March"? The list is a virtual "Who's Who" of every freakhouse liberal organization in America. The NAACP; the National Organization for Women (New York); Bilingual Foundation of the Arts; National Education Association; Handgun Control, Inc.; the Coalition to Stop Handgun Violence; National Council of Churches; 100 Blacks Police Officers Against Violence; National League of Women Voters; Physicians for Social Responsibility; Mothers Against Violence in America; American Jewish Congress; National PTA; and on and on and on.

The list now tops 100 and every name on it reeks of left-wing fanaticism.

Mother's Day is one of the most important days of the year. Hopefully, it won't be totally desecrated by this march of a million nuts.

Wendy's Massacre Thanks to Gun Control

In the wake of the unspeakable execution-style murders at Wendy's, gun control advocates must be very satisfied with themselves today. They must be very pleased indeed.

The seven victims, tied up with duct tape, plastic bags placed around their heads, their faces pressed against the cold cellar floor, were vanquished in cold blood, their brains blown out by an illegal .380-caliber semiautomatic. If only we had strict gun control.

But wait! What's that? We *do* have tight gun control? And *still* these people were killed? How the hell did that happen?

These crimes were committed in New York City by residents of New York City, a place more than synonymous with gun control. Relative to the rest of the country, New York's gun control laws border on prohibition. Only Washington, D.C. — affectionately known as the murder capital of America — has stricter gun control than New York.

Americans frequently hear about battles over waiting periods. Should they be three days? Five days? Seven days? Different states have varying waiting periods, a pet panacea of gun control fanatics. California gun controllers boast about their 15 day waiting period. In New York City, there is a *six to eight month* waiting period. In New York, it is practically a crime to even look at a gun.

Gun controllers are undoubtedly shocked that their precious gun control laws didn't work at Wendy's in Flushing, Queens. They are shocked because they are fools. Gun control never works. The prohibitionists are dumbfounded that the Wendy's murderers, John Taylor and Craig Godineaux, were not deterred by New York's gun control laws. These two misfit career criminals, who specialized in the armed robberies of fast food restaurants, did not purchase their weapon from a licensed dealer (a favorite target of gun controllers.) They did not submit to a background check. No waiting period for John Taylor.

Gun control, however, did play a part in the Wendy's massacre, however. It played a very crucial part indeed. Thanks to New York's gun control laws, Wendy's manager Jean Auguste was forced to tie up his workers. Entrusted with their lives, this poor man never had the option of self-defense. At gunpoint, he bound his employees with duct tape before having his own brains blown out. If only he had his own equalizer.

Ramon Nazario and Anita Smith (what in God's name could have been going through their minds?) also felt the naked brutal reality of defenselessness moments before their deaths. John Taylor and Craig Godineaux, if they have any sense whatsoever, certainly must be eternally grateful for the gun control laws that allowed them free rein, without a threat to their actions. It is axiomatic that career criminals are the strongest supporters of tight control. Hardened street hoodlums simply do not want to carry out their trade in locales where honest people are armed. This is not only common sense, it has been proven beyond the shadow of a doubt, despite the hysterical and unbearably shrill whines of rubber-headed gun controllers.

The great Charlton Heston, president of the National Rifle Association, has explained his conversion from Hollywood liberal to sober-minded thinker by describing the mentality he frequently encountered from the lefties in his business. Liberals, he explains, would always justify their political positions with emotion-based rationale, never common sense or a cold look at facts. Nuclear arms control, like gun control, was defended by his colleagues as a "gut issue." Don't bother us with the facts. It feels good, so let's do it.

Douglas Montero, a liberal columnist with the *New York Post*, actually went to the trouble of speaking to store owners in the same neighborhood as Wendy's. In a surprisingly thoughtful piece,

Montero imparted the stories of shopkeepers whose lives were saved in the midst of robberies by the presence of their own firearms. Garfield Hart, proprietor of an electronics store, pumped a bullet into the chest of an armed bandit with his life-saving equalizer. No plastic bag over Garfield Hart's head. He's alive.

Lilly Fu, 27 years old, fired a shot into the neck of a career hoodlum, shooting him dead outside her boyfriend's cell phone business in Flushing, Queens. Montero writes, "Fu and Hart could have conceivably been registered as statistics, like the victims at Wendy's who were led to a basement freezer, bound with duct tape and killed like dogs." Instead, thanks to guns in the hands of honest people, the real dogs are dead, snuffed out like the vermin they are.

Throughout America, hundreds of thousands of lives are saved and crimes prevented each year because of the presence of guns in the hands of law-abiding citizens. Over the past decade, "right to carry" laws enacted in many states have enabled citizens to carry concealed weapons — all to the horror of street predators. Crime in those locales has plummeted.

But never mind. Gun controllers will continue to ignore reality and scream for more gun control, while ignoring the screams of the Wendy's victims, where a gun in the hands of one of them would have saved their lives.

Put McGruff to Sleep

McGruff, the alleged crime-fighting canine famous for his Columbo-style raincoat and the slogan, "Take a bite out of crime," first made his bones as the mascot for the National Crime Prevention Council (NCPC). As he became more famous, McGruff began appearing live at the various "Night Out Against Crime" festivals and, taking a break from his Santa Claus suit, would be photographed with every smiling politician.

But this dog, despite his reputation, is clearly not "man's best friend." In fact, as the barking advocate against the right to bear arms and the howling shill for removing legally owned firearms from the homes of honest citizens, McGruff can more accurately be called the "criminal's best friend." It is time to put McGruff to sleep.

The NCPC is a taxpayer-funded federal agency, which, under the guise of an advisory council and public interest advocacy body, actually functions as a mouthpiece for the most notorious anti-gun organizations in America. So McGruff, in reality, has evolved into a quasi-employee for the very groups that are most helpful to America's criminal element. This is on the order of Smokey the Bear making public service announcements for the advancement of pyromania.

The brochure put out by the NCPC, "Dealing With Gun Violence," is nothing more than a propaganda sheet for gun-banning fanatics. In it, McGruff steals the message of Eddie Eagle, the mascot of the National Rifle Association's child gun safety program — "Stop, Don't Touch, Get Away, Tell a Grown-Up You Trust" — which is the only sensible point in the pamphlet, since imitation is the highest form of flattery. But McGruff, of course, goes further, advocating the complete *removal* of guns from homes with children.

This mixed up mutt also advises, "Ask local officials to advocate a variety of ways to prevent handgun violence, such as increasing local regulation of those with Federal Firearms Licenses, consumer protection regulations governing manufacture, taxes on ammunition, bans on so-called 'assault weapons,' gun turn-in days and liability legislation."

Whew! That'll do the trick! Crack down on law-abiding people and inanimate objects. Rumor has it that Chuck Schumer has been spotted running into a phone booth just before McGruff appears on the scene. (In fact, the "gun turn-in" charade is actually one of the more hilarious inventions of the anti-gun movement. The basic idea is that, given some public-spirited incentive such as free Yankee tickets or an autographed picture of Cindy Crawford, hardened criminals will surrender with amnesty the very weapons they were about to use to rob a bank. The program even embarrasses most gun banners.)

The brochure also lists three "organizations" to contact for more information: The Center for Handgun Violence, Coalition to Stop Gun Violence and the National School Safety Center. All of these groups are staunch proponents of eliminating the right to bear arms and of cracking down on the gun-availability to law-abiding citizens. Nowhere in their literature do they distinguish the honest firearm owner from the gun-toting mugger. And nowhere in the brochure does McGruff propose that criminal perpetrators be locked up and given strict prison sentences.

This grotesque misuse of the American tax dollar is part of the larger abominable and tyrannical trend on the part of the Clinton Administration to conduct a regulatory war on the Second Amendment. Using government agencies, rather than the legislative process, to snatch away freedoms is the new and very efficient method of accomplishing the anti-gun agenda without having to face the will of the voters.

The awesome power of an unrestrained federal government is the certain road to totalitarianism. This back door method of abolishing freedoms has manifested itself not only through the NCPC, but the Bureau of Alcohol, Tobacco and Firearms (BATF), which has dramatically cut the lawful availability of all firearms by strangling commerce. BATF simply will not license honest dealers, decreasing their number by close to half since 1993.

Clinton has also given broad power to ban ammunition to the Treasury Department, which will eventually result in the ban of rifles used for hunting, target shooting and personal protection. The Federal Trade Commission (FTC) has pressed for a ban on firearm advertising. Ignoring that guns are used successfully for self-defense more than two million times per year, the FTC has labeled firearm ads "false and misleading" on the topic of personal defense. The White House has also used the Department of Defense, the Environmental Protection Agency (EPA), the Department of the Interior and even international agencies such as the United Nations and the Arms Control and Disarmament Agency (ACDA) to issue myriads of rulings and regulations designed to obstruct, interfere, and eventually prohibit the private ownership of firearms.

Even the Center for Disease Control, which views firearms as a "germ" that must be eradicated, is being used as a propaganda machine for the anti-gun movement. Before these monstrosities metastasize further, McGruff ought to be neutered or, even better, put out of his misery, as a fair warning.

Some "Hate Crimes" More Equal Than Others

The biggest news in New York City last week concerned an event which took place in Casper, Wyoming. This same event was also the front-page news in Albuquerque, New Mexico and, for that matter, in Juneau, Alaska. Although more than 20,000 murders take place in the United States every year, the grisly killing of Matthew Shepard became national news not because he is any more dead than the others, but because of the alleged *motivation* of his killers. Shepard, as anyone tracking the news knows, was murdered during a robbery, but emerged as a national figure because he was also slain for being a homosexual.

Amidst the whirlwind of national publicity, collective soul-searching and breast-beating, the President of the United States, the Governor of the State of New York and every other pandering politician has called on every branch and level of government to pass "hate crimes" legislation which would, once again, declare one's sexual behavior to be a specially privileged and protected right. President Clinton sent two representatives to the Shepard funeral, including Sean Maloney, the highest ranking homosexual in his administration.

Another "hate crime" receiving the same level of attention occurred almost as recently in Jasper, Texas, where a black man, James Byrd, was tortured and murdered, his body tied to a pick-up truck and dragged mercilessly through the streets. So horrific was the crime that a New York City police officer was fired for his involvement in a parody of the incident, where several men in blackface dragged a dummy as part of a parade float. Again, the Byrd incident gained national attention for the crime's impetus, not for the result. In response to both the Shepard and Byrd murders, Bill Clinton used his national radio address as a forum to discuss these cases.

The idea of "hate crimes" legislation is preposterous on its face. The entire notion is predicated on the ridiculous axiom that what a person *thinks* as opposed to what he *does* should warrant greater punishment simply because the Thought Police deem certain ideas particularly reprehensible. That a perpetrator who vandalizes and sets fire to a store should receive less punishment because he was angry that the cashier short-changed him yesterday — as opposed to committing the crime while spouting racial slurs — is logic that only the mind of a totalitarian could be comfortable with. The entire "hate crimes" movement is merely a clever ruse to the eventual enactment of speech codes and imprisonment, not for "hateful" acts, but for similar *speech* and similar *thoughts*.

Notwithstanding the tyrannical agenda of the proponents of this ghastly threat to freedom is the transparency of their ideology. It seems that only certain categories of "victims" are worthy of presidential proclamations and national attention. Indeed, as George Orwell would say, some "hate crimes" are more equal than others.

Last month, shortly before the Shepard murder, two white girls, Tracy Lambert and Susan Moore, were murdered as part of a racially-motivated initiation of new members into the Black and Hispanic Crips gang in Fayetteville, North Carolina. In Denver, 14 year old Brandy Duvall was abducted from a bus stop by the Black and Hispanic Bloods gang. Gang member Francisco Martinez and six other members took young Brandy to one of their houses where they spent several hours raping her and torturing her sexually with a knife and a broomstick.

Martinez laughed repeatedly as he rammed the broomstick into Brandy while she screamed and pleaded for her life. When the gang was finished with her, Brandy was stabbed 28 times and her body was dumped in a ditch. Back in Fayetteville, a 25 year old white soldier named Donald Lange was dragged into a parking lot by a group of black soldiers, stomped and beaten as they hurled racial epithets at him. Lange was beaten so severely that doctors have declared him a vegetable beyond recovery. Witnesses have testified that Lange was kicked nearly to death despite pleas by bystanders to leave him alone.

Of course, no one outside Fayetteville or Denver has ever heard of Tracy Lambert, Susan Moore, Brandy Duvall or Donald Lange. They were not mentioned during the President's weekly radio address. Administration officials were not sent to their funerals. Politicians have not campaigned on their graves. There have been no calls for a crackdown on the "causes" of non-white racism. No breast-beating. No marches or rallies. No updates and talking heads on Nightline. In fact, if whites actually shocked the world and demonstrated against this most common of interracial violence, the only racism denounced would undoubtedly be that of the demonstrators.

The instances of black on white brutality are too many to enumerate. Yet media and politicians create a national din only when the politically correct victim groups are on the wrong side of the violence. If the races of the victims and perpetrators in Fayetteville and Denver were reversed, they likely would have bumped Matthew Shepard off the front pages. Instead, "hate crimes" continue to be defined by liberal political standards, not on the basis of which race is actually committing the preponderance of crimes and which race is most victimized, but by the agenda of radical interest groups, with ivory tower white complicity.

Kennesaw Embarrasses Gun Controllers

Kennesaw, Georgia, USA deserves to be the capital of the United States. The Southern city historically best-known for producing the legendary judge and baseball commissioner "Kennesaw Mountain" Landis, has reached a milestone that has liberal gun control advocates shaking their heads in passive aggressive denial. What has been revealed of Kennesaw is certainly not news that's "fit to print." On second thought, perhaps Kennesaw is a rather poor choice for the nation's capital. Crime in that proud polity is, antithetically to Washington, D.C., so distressingly low.

It is axiomatic to all Americans of the most minimal common sense that guns in the hands of law-abiding citizens is the greatest deterrent to street crime. The trend is an absolute. In locales where citizens freely carry guns, crime is lowest. In metropolises with tight gun control, violent crime is rampant. The reasons for this are so self-evident they hardly need explaining. Why would a criminal want to mug someone who has a gun? In fact, why would a street thug want to attack anyone in a city where people are, by law, permitted to carry firearms? The potential prey *might* have a gun. To a well-thinking criminal, the most bountiful terrain for a life of crime is a city with strong gun control laws, where the predator *knows* people are unarmed.

This, of course, is all so much basic logic. But not to gun control fanatics, who simultaneously deny the obvious and ignore all relevant statistics on such matters. Moreover, in addition to their troubling ignorance, gun controllers are among the most shameless liars. Still further, gun controllers actually maintain, with a straight face, the notion that gun control is an *anti-crime* measure. This is on the order of death penalty abolitionists claiming that capital punishment is not only not a deterrent, but actually *encourages* murder.

Kennesaw, and the news made public two weeks ago, now presents gun control enthusiasts with an unbearable and embarrassing situation because the city takes the extraordinary step of not only allowing law-abiding persons to possess a gun, but *requiring* it.

On March 25, 1982, Kennesaw enacted an ordinance requiring law-abiding heads of households to keep at least one firearm in their homes. Subsequent to that law, which is now celebrating its 19th anniversary, the population of Kennesaw rose from somewhat over 5,000 to about 15,000 today. But the most stunning numbers (to gun controllers, not to sensible people) are the plummeting crime statistics in response to the law. In the very first year of its enactment, violent crimes dropped 74 percent. They fell another 45 percent in the second year. Even with the rising population, the crime numbers have stayed unbelievably low.

The homicide rate is now non-existent. There have been exactly three murders in 19 years — two with knives and one with a gun. Yes, all those legally accessible guns haven't exactly spurred honest people to mayhem, as gun controllers would claim. (Maybe the two knife murders will have them calling for knife control, since the knife-murder rate is double the gun-murder rate!)

Other crimes of violence have also virtually disappeared from the radar screen in Kennesaw. The average number of armed robberies is 1.69 per year; rapes average two per year. Burglaries into people's homes are basically suicide missions for criminals. And what is significant is that it appears that the *mere presence* of firearms or, more importantly, the *advance knowledge* that Kennesaw citizens are armed, has prevented criminals from even trying.

Now, it would seem in a country with a free press, especially one that is prone to publicize occurrences that it considers staggering, that the news out of Kennesaw would be front-page and network-leading. Don't bet on it. Major media are so married to the gun control philosophy that their transparent bias will not permit the same kind of attention given to schoolyard killings that invariably result in worried editorials calling for more gun control.

So, with the results coming out of Kennesaw mirroring what has occurred in every other part of the country where guns reside in the hands of honest people, why haven't national politicians pointed to the facts as an excuse for abolishing America's 20,000 worthless gun control laws? Interestingly, gun control proved such a losing issue in 2000 for liberals that its usual proponents, like Senator Chuck Schumer, were conspicuously silent after the recent Santee school shooting. In fact, Schumer was not exactly silent — he issued a statement saying he would not use the incident as a reason for introducing more gun control legislation. Progress,

progress.

It is said in certain circles that if so-called civil libertarians were as passionate about defending the Second Amendment as they are about the First, college professors would be making speeches insisting the Second Amendment requires mandatory gun ownership. Kennesaw, Georgia is ahead of its time.

Gun Buyback Program a Sham

The capacity on the part of liberals to devise outlandish policies intended to combat crime is rivaled in stupidity only by their propensity to avoid true solutions. Gun control has always been the pet panacea of those who possess neither the desire nor the backbone to confront the true and obvious cause of gun violence: criminals and a lenient justice system. Rather than confront this bane head on, gun controllers have striven to crack down on their favorite whipping boys, the guns themselves.

Every time another maniac opens fire, the calls goes out for stricter gun control. Gun controllers, however, never quite get around to explaining how the previous 20,000 gun control laws they enthusiastically enacted failed to stop the most recent tragedies. The most recent shootings in the Los Angeles Jewish center and the Texas shooting in a Christian church were not — and could not — have been prevented by existing gun control laws. Nevertheless, the reaction has been typical and predictable.

In the short time in between these shootings, President Clinton latched onto and actually expanded what is probably the nuttiest (although not the most harmful) policy that is aimed at guns rather than criminals. In what is generally referred to as "gun buyback" programs, the President has taken a page from local communities around the country and announced a $15 million federal plan which will assist local authorities in purchasing firearms in and around public housing projects.

In the past, gun buyback programs work like this: police in a local neighborhood or precinct, often with the assistance of misguided community organizations, announce that they want people to turn in their illegal (or legal) guns. A period of amnesty is offered, whereby anyone who owns a weapon illegally will not be punished or prosecuted if they hand in the gun within the allotted time frame. No questions asked. Sometimes, the buyback program operates under the condition of anonymity of the illegal gun owner. (There is no amnesty for crimes committed with guns.)

In exchange for turning in their guns, people will receive a determined amount of cash. Sometimes, they are offered basketball tickets or some other desirable item. Amidst great hoopla, the program is announced under the guise of an "anti-gun" program. Since people will be turning in their guns, and guns cause crime, ipso facto, crime will be reduced.

The only effect that these ridiculous programs have on criminals is that certain robberies may be delayed while the muggers try to stop laughing. The entire program is predicated on the nonsensical notion that criminals are the ones that turn in their guns. That an IQ above 10 could actually take such logic seriously is one of the great mysteries of life. But, alas, some people actually purport to believe it.

The Clinton program is aimed at reducing gun violence in some of the most notoriously dangerous locations in America. It will give local police departments up to $500,000 each to purchase guns for a "suggested price" of $50. "Every gun turned in through a buyback program means potentially one less tragedy," Clinton profoundly exclaims.

Clinton, who certainly inspires confidence when he asserts that the guns will be destroyed upon receipt by the police, calculates that the new program will bring in roughly 300,000 guns. The federal money will go to individual public housing authorities which will coordinate plans with local police. The Clinton administration has come up with the novel idea that gift certificates for goods or services be handed out instead of cash. Very appealing to the neighborhood mugger.

Naturally, when reality actually manages to break through the clouds of deception, the facts reveal that there is no evidence whatsoever that crime has been reduced in locales where gun buyback programs have been enacted. This is in line with the fact that crime does not go down in areas which establish more gun control laws. In fact, the only places where crime decreases are where right-to-carry laws are passed — laws which make it easier for law-abiding citizens to carry concealed weapons for self-protection.

The Associated Press reports that the thousands of weapons turned in through buyback programs over the years hardly make a dent in the 220 million to 250 million guns in circulation. The people who turn in the guns are undoubtedly comprised of those not committing crimes and people who simply want to get rid of their guns anyway. Obviously, criminals who make their living breaking laws with guns are not interested in surrendering the tools of the trade for a gift certificate.

But public policy is rarely based on logic and common sense.

Racial Profiling is Justified

"Racial profiling" is the newest hot-button topic in the United States. In a country with some of the strangest public obsessions, racial profiling encompasses two of America's most pressing problems, race and crime. Opposition to racial profiling is the new pet panacea of the anti-racist jihad. Police departments throughout America are being confronted by the racial bloodhounds, determined to root out this sinister practice wherever it might be. It is rampant, they say, and must be eradicated, like slavery, segregation, Jim Crow and the bubonic plague.

In the case of racial profiling, the crusade to eliminate it is not merely the province of liberals. In fact, there is not one conservative politician in America who would defend it. There are no police departments that admit to practicing it or would defend it if it was found to be permeating their officers' tactics. Unlike affirmative action or racial set-asides, there are not two *public* sides to racial profiling. *Everyone* says it's wrong and *everyone* states that it must be ended.

No less a conservative than Attorney General John Ashcroft has made himself the leading public advocate for the elimination of racial profiling. With the complete vocal support of President Bush, Ashcroft has stated, "It's wrong and it must be ended. No matter how rare it is, it's like unemployment in that to the unemployed person it's 100 percent. To the person who's wrongly stopped, racial profiling is 100 percent."

The phenomenon called "racial profiling" was given its name after a scandal of sorts broke out in 1998 regarding the actions of the New Jersey State Police, who were said to have stopped blacks as suspects more often than whites. From there it mushroomed into a national issue, with presidential candidate Al Gore beating up his opponent, New Jersey Senator Bill Bradley, for the racial profiling that made such hay in Bradley's home state. More recently, New York City Mayor Rudy Giuliani has gone ballistic at the notion that his cops practice racial profiling. The only thing that separates the anti-racist Left from moderates and conservatives on the issue is their belief in exactly how widespread racial profiling is. The liberals think it's everywhere; the rest say it's quite rare.

All of this posturing, of course, is very strange. For the only thing that the anti-racist Left is correct about is that racial profiling *is* quite rampant. Virtually all police departments *do* practice it. The fact is that any police department worth its salt *necessarily must* practice racial profiling. It is, quite simply, the most professional and effective way for the police to do their jobs.

Privately, cops will admit that they engage in racial profiling. In fact, they practice many forms of profiling — age, gender, dress, and behavioral nuance profiling. The FBI practices profiling (a television series called "Profiler" was based on it), which is why they target single white males as serial killers. The generic single white male has committed no crime, yet the FBI focuses on and watches them more closely because the statistics don't lie. This group is simply most likely to have a serial killer within it. If the FBI swore to examine and pursue each and every demographic group equally in pursuit of serial killers they could not do their jobs properly.

The police are in exactly the same position. Their experience — and all government crime data — tells them that men are more violent than women and to an overwhelming extent are more likely to commit crimes. Police, therefore, stop and focus on men much more than women in pursuit of violent criminals. Experience also tells them that young men are more violent than older men. And, what experience tells them more profoundly than anything else, is that young black men are much more violent than any other demographic group. If the police ignored this reality, dismissed their own training and experience, they too could not do their jobs effectively.

If an idealistic rookie cop determined that he would be guided by what passes for today's wisdom and would, therefore, treat and react to every demographic group equally — and would stop and focus on little old Asian women as often as young black men — he would soon realize that he was wasting his time and doing an ineffective job as a cop.

The American intelligentsia has placed an unfair and insurmountable burden on police officers. It wants them to catch criminals, but insists that they ignore the entire gestalt of their experience. It tells them to ignore the fact that blacks are eight times more likely to commit crimes of violence than whites; that blacks commit 90 percent of the interracial crimes of violence in America; and that, as a stunning statistical matter, blacks are as much more violent than whites, as men are more violent than women.

Men are stopped more frequently by police than women, yet no one cries "gender profiling" because it is accepted that men simply commit more crimes than women. The police are doing exactly what they should be doing. From a statistical point of view, they are just as justified stopping blacks more than whites.

Last week in New York City, police stopped a man they suspected was armed when they saw him running at night, holding his hip. The man's actions were not a crime, but the cops were using their experience which told them he might be armed. They were profiling. And they were right.

The Church and the Death Penalty

Excepting the painful issue of abortion, on which the Roman Catholic Church has maintained a steadfastness in complete opposition to its practice, the Church, on the various "social issues," has for decades wallowed in a swamp of hopeless liberalism. An inordinate number of the Church hierarchy — from the Pope to the bishops to the parish priests — have sought to impart the bizarre notion that in order to be a Catholic in good standing, one must adhere to the liberal drivel that emanates from the bowels of the Church's oversensitized social compass.

Indeed, the Church's pronouncements on the obligatory welfare state and the righteousness of the transfer of wealth, as well as its open borders stance on immigration have given it the well-deserved image as a bastion of rabid and implacable leftism. It is distressing that both John Paul II and the recently departed Cardinal John O'Connor — the Church's most influential spokesmen — were jealous guardians of these views.

But what are individual Catholics to make of this liberal morass? What are Catholic obligations of obedience to these pronouncements? What is doctrine? What is dogma? What are merely opinions and suggestions? And finally, what is the "infallibility" of Church statements?

While most people believe that the Catholic Church is vociferously opposed to capital punishment, the fact remains that opposition to the death penalty is not official doctrine. In recent years, John Paul and Cardinal O'Connor have criticized its imposition as adding to the "culture of death." In recent decades, the Catholic Bishops have also issued public statements in opposition to the death penalty. In fairness, they have not claimed that such opposition is official teaching, nor have they denied the compatibility of the death penalty with the Catholic faith. Nevertheless, confusion among Catholics stems from the tortured line between Church statements and Church doctrine.

In 1980, the Catholic bishops issued a statement which said in part, "Allowing for the fact that Catholic teaching has accepted the principle that the state has the right to take the life of a person guilty of an extremely serious crime, and that the state may take appropriate measures to protect itself and its citizens from grave harm, nevertheless, the question for judgment and decision today is whether capital punishment is justifiable under present circumstances."

While this was clearly a thoughtful statement which made a heroic effort to justify moral opposition to the death penalty, it is painfully obvious that plain, worn-out liberalism was the crucial factor in the conclusion the bishops reached. The "present circumstances" of 1980 just happened to be the time when the death penalty was never *more* justifiable, given the explosion in the American national murder rate, a trend which has since stabilized but which is still enormously high by historical standards.

In 1952, Pope Pius XII said, "Even when it is a question of the execution of a man condemned to death, the state does not dispose of the individual's right to live. Rather, it is reserved to the public authority to deprive the criminal of the benefit of life, when already, by his crime, he has *deprived himself* of the right to live." (Emphasis added.)

The Fifth Commandment, "Thou Shall Not Kill," is often cited by death penalty opponents as the definitive source of Christian thinking on capital punishment. However, the Catechism of the Council of Trent stated, "Another kind of slaying is permitted, which belongs to those magistrates to whom is given the power of condemning to death, by legal and judicial use of which [power] they punish the guilty and protect the innocent (Rom. 13:4)... as the proposed end of this law [The Fifth Commandment] is to provide for the life and safety of men, to the same end also tend the punishments [executions] inflicted by the magistrates, who are the legitimate avengers of crimes, giving security to life by punishing and thus repressing audacity and outrage."

It would be practically impossible, given today's political climate, for current churchmen to issue such a forthright statement in defense of capital punishment. But whatever side one is one, it is obvious that the proponents of the death penalty were guided more by Scripture than personal opinion, and that today's opponents (not necessarily including the Pope) are more guided by political correctness and droopy liberalism.

Today's Catholic opposition to capital punishment does not fall into the category of doctrine, dogma or the more extreme "infallible" statement, which can deal only with matters of revelation and salvation and can be expressed only "ex cathedra" — official teaching. (Only two infallible statements have been made in the past two centuries: the immaculate conception of Mary in 1854 — that she was conceived without original sin; and the bodily assumption of Mary into heaven, in 1950.) According to "Catholicism Today: A Survey of Catholic Belief and Practice," Church statements on the death penalty should be received with "respect and docility" by the faithful, but are not binding.

Finally, what would Jesus's position be today? As One who was the recipient of the death penalty, He would undoubtedly possess a unique perspective. It is probably safe to assume that He would scoff at the political correctness of today — as He did in His day — and remain the loyal Servant to Scripture that He always was.

True Feminine Protection

Would you shoot a rapist before he slits your throat?

If the zany women who participated in this year's Million Nut March have their way, you won't even have the chance. Yes, for the second straight year, Mother's Day has been tainted by that bizarre concoction, the so-called "Million Mom March," a gathering of "concerned" mothers whose function is to call for yet more gun control laws as a way of stopping violence.

This peculiar phenomenon, launched in 2000, ostensibly in response to high-profile shooting incidents, has fallen, thankfully, flat on its face. The entire gun control movement was a disaster for its proponents in the 2000 elections, with even anti-gun luminaries like Senators Bob Torricelli and Chuck Schumer backing off. But stark reality and a rational look at the facts has never been much of a motivator for the leftist organizers of the Million Nut March.

They are, in fact, marching straight to their own murders and rapes if their totalitarian philosophy prevails. Right now, the staunchest supporters of the anti-gun, anti-self-defense agenda of the Million Nut March are the assorted muggers, rapists and predators in American society. Organizers of the March are still oblivious to the sight of hardened street criminals cheering them on. The ignorance of the organizers is quite profound indeed.

Violence against women in America is frighteningly commonplace. A Department of Justice survey found that roughly 40 percent of prisoners had a "criminal justice status" (on probation, parole or under a restraining order) at the time of their most recent crime against their wives or girlfriends. Almost 1.5 million women are raped or physically assaulted by an intimate partner every year in the United States. The survey also found that 52 percent of women at some time had been the victim of an assault. These are astounding numbers.

So what is it that can provide true feminine protection? If the trends are any indication, it is the fact that 17 million women in America now own guns, and the number is climbing.

Contrary to liberal reportage, there are many feminine voices of common sense which are countering the bombast of the Million Nuts. Second Amendment Sisters, a pro-gun women's organization, has organized rallies in several states as a means of advocating the right of self-defense, not the right to be defenseless. They state, "A restraining order waved at an enraged 'ex' has not been proven an effective means of self-defense; neither has a telephone receiver in one hand... If you are a woman who owns a gun, you have an equalizer. Since most assailants will be bigger and stronger than you, and almost 90 percent of those assailants will not have a weapon of their own, you stand a much better chance of getting away unscathed if you are armed. Isn't that your right?"

Liz Michael writes, "The so-called 'Million Mom March' represents a clear and present danger to every woman in this nation, especially every teenage girl in this nation. Every woman participating in this march is participating in an act that may very well lead to her own death, assault, or rape, as well as the death, assault or rape of any woman or young girl in her family. Every individual participating in this march or financing this march is effectively sponsoring a future criminal assault on me and people I love, and I hold them as responsible as the criminal himself."

She continues, "The 'Million Mugger-enabling Meddlers'... aren't trying to make it safe for my kid to walk the street. They're actually setting up situations where my family might be rendered defenseless against these same thugs."

Therein lies the most important point about the Million Nuts. They are not merely stupid; they are enablers. And it is perfect common sense that rapists would be cheering on their actions. But as the trends show, the Million Nuts are losing ground, not gaining. Women are arming themselves at record rates. Not only are groups like Second Amendment Sisters forming, but there are now magazines catering to women and self-defense — self-defense with firearms, not restraining orders.

Diane Alden writes, "Moms with guns are a lot better off than moms who wait for 911. What are you going to do when someone breaks into your home? A. Call Rosie O'Donnell and tell her to come over and nag the crooks to death. B. Wait 30 minutes for the police to show up while your ex-husband is breaking through the door screaming, 'If I can't have you, no one will.' C. Tell the bad guys that they are breaking 28,000 gun laws, then show them chapter and verse. D. Write down the bad guy's life story for a Barbara Walters special while commiserating with him on his miserable childhood."

It is heartening that the American Constitution, particularly the Second Amendment, is taken so seriously by sober-minded women. If the Million Nuts want disarmament, make it unilateral and allow right-thinking women the opportunity to stay alive.

Racial Profiling Lives!

Stop the presses. Even the liberal media cannot suppress this news.

In the wake of the greatest disaster in American history and the attendant loss of innocent life in the heart of the United States, a return to common sense is manifesting itself. As several polls now reveal, the public -- especially American blacks -- supports racial profiling.

While several newspaper articles and television interviews have provided anecdotal testimony demonstrating a wariness toward Arab or Moslem-looking people, particularly in groups and in airports, it is the most recent Gallup poll that has stunned the elitist intelligentsia. According to Gallup, an astonishing 71 percent of blacks stated that racial profiling is justified and that they practice it. Fully 59 percent of whites said they support it. These findings are startling because it has been widely assumed that blacks -- who are most often the target of racial profiling -- are the most adamantly opposed to the practice. That the poll shows a greater support for racial profiling by blacks than whites is nothing less than stunning.

While it may be that 41 percent of whites are merely lying and are afraid to tell the truth on such a delicate question, it cannot be overstated the significance that blacks support profiling in such high numbers. It has always been an absolute fact that Americans of all races practice racial profiling. This is just so much common sense. Black cab drivers are themselves notorious for refusing to pick up black male passengers for fear of being killed.

It is only politicians and high-level police officials who see the need to pretend that racial profiling is wrong and ought to be condemned. In fact, policemen would lose their jobs for admitting the obvious -- that they, of course, practice it, too. Every cop knows he couldn't possibly do his job effectively without using the entire gestalt of his experience -- which means practicing racial profiling.

For once, Al Sharpton was tongue-tied. It was truly a sight to behold. Presented with this overwhelming black support for racial profiling, Sharpton responded, "I don't care if 100 percent of blacks are for it, it would still be wrong and I'd still be against it."

Black radio announcer Ken Hamblin, naturally, was more sensible on the subject. "What it shows," Hamblin said, "is that black people are just like everyone else. They are afraid of being victims and will use their common sense and judgement to protect themselves."

A representative of a newly formed Moslem group decries the findings, comparing Americans' trepidation at the sight of Arabs to women holding their purses closer to their bodies when they see young black men. Clearly, this person is in denial. Why, she continued, were whites not profiled after Timothy McVeigh was found to have blown up the federal building in Oklahoma? In fact, profiling did occur -- immediately. Profiling against members of militia groups was widely undertaken by the government, even though these people had done nothing wrong.

Prior to the release of the stunning Gallup poll results, the *New York Times* began paving the way for public acknowledgment of the racial profiling issue in a thoughtful front-page article entitled, "Once Appalled by Race Profiling, Many Find Themselves Doing It." In a series of discussions with a group of non-whites, the *Times* revealed the pragmatic impact of the terrorist attacks on ordinary Americans.

The article began, "Ron Arnold understands racial profiling. 'I'm a black American, and I've been racially profiled all my life... and it's wrong.' But Mr. Arnold admits he is engaging in some racial profiling himself these days, casting a wary eye on men who look to be of Middle Eastern descent. If he saw a small knot of such men boarding a plane on which he was about to fly, he said: 'Yes, I'd be aware of them. I'd be nervous. It sickens me that I feel that way, but it's the real world.'"

Adrian Estala, a Hispanic man from Houston, told the *Times*, "Absolutely I have to be honest... Yes, it would make me second-guess. Anybody that says no, they're a better man than I am, or a better woman. I would feel nervous. I mean, who wouldn't?"

Indeed, these sentiments, revealed both in the *New York Times* and the Gallup poll, reflect nothing deep or penetratingly psychological. They reflect the normal workings of the minds of average people unencumbered by political nonsense.

Moreover, racial and ethnic profiling (as well as age, dress, and gender profiling) are effective tools for both law enforcement and civilians. People profile all the times in their own lives and when making common sense judgements. It is quite revealing that a special effort must be made to *prevent* people from racial profiling. That such an effort is necessary is an admission that people practice it spontaneously as a matter of course. To not engage in profiling is against human nature, not the other way around. Finally, some honesty on the subject is making its way into public discourse. A shame that it took the toppling of two towers to do it.

V

PROFILES

Hide Your Guns From Schumer

Honest law-abiding firearm owners, and other menaces to society, have become especially exhausted since election night when Congressman Chuck Schumer was elected to the United States Senate. That is because they have spent every waking hour hiding their guns from him.

Much was made during the campaign against incumbent Alphonse D'Amato about Schumer's position on the House Judiciary Committee, where he cast his vote to shield Bill Clinton from impeachment. It was during the height of those debates that the name Peter Rodino, the congressman from New Jersey, was resurrected from the past. Rodino, now retired and in his late eighties, was the chairman of the judiciary committee during the Nixon era and conducted the Watergate hearings.

Suddenly back in the public eye, Rodino received daily accolades for his supposed fairness and statesmanship during Watergate. That is the Peter Rodino that is now remembered and will be recorded by history. But that is not the Peter Rodino that firearm owners remember. Rodino was, in fact, the original Chuck Schumer.

As the leading anti-gun activist in the House, Rodino brazenly announced in 1984 that the McClure-Volkmer bill, which had already passed the Senate and would reform some of the most egregious provisions of the Gun Control Act of 1968, was "dead on arrival." He vowed to never even give the bill a hearing, thus preventing it from being voted on and, essentially, killing it. Even some anti-gun Democrats resented Rodino's dictatorial stance. In a scarcely used procedure, the House voted on a discharge position, thereby circumventing Rodino and allowing a vote of the full House. The bill passed and was signed by President Reagan.

In recent years, Schumer has filled Rodino's shoes amply and has emerged as the most notorious gun banner in the Congress. Now, as a United States Senator, Schumer is a bigger and more powerful fish in a smaller pond. His reign of terror will begin January 1. And unlike most anti-gun politicians who are so ignorant of the issue that they do not know a semi-automatic from a wrist watch, Schumer is extraordinarily knowledgeable, extremely effective and very smart. Still, somehow, he cannot count to two. He has never heard of the Second Amendment. His new nick-name is "The Confiscator." He wants your guns.

Schumer was the most ardent advocate of the Brady Law, which requires, among other things, a waiting period for a law-abiding citizen to purchase a weapon for self-defense. On the day the bill became law, Schumer called a press conference and declared that Brady wouldn't do all he had previously said it would do to stop crime. As usual, when the gun banners get what they want, they then announce that the just-passed regulation is only a "small step." Much more is always needed. Waiting periods become longer. Background checks more cumbersome. All small steps on the road to gun confiscation.

Schumer has also been at the forefront of the "assault weapons" ban. Now, no one has yet figured out exactly what an "assault weapon" is, but even by Congress' definition, these rifles have been used in *one tenth of one percent* of all gun crimes. And that's setting aside the fact that only the law-abiding are even hurt by the law. Even the virulently anti-gun Bureau of Alcohol, Tobacco and Firearms testified that the ban would do nothing to stop crime.

Schumer is now the nation's driving force behind Brady II, the sequel. He supports national identification and registration for all gun owners — the better to confiscate them at government's whim. Transferring ownership from one citizen to another without government involvement will eventually be illegal. As part of Brady II, Schumer is pushing for special taxes on firearm owners and as part of licensing fees to have these honest citizens pay for damages caused by gun violence and gun crimes.

In other words, according to Schumer, a certain group of people should be forced to pay for consequences of actions *they did not commit*. This is on the order of taxing people who buy matches and charcoal to barbecue — to pay for the crimes committed by arsonists.

Gun controllers like Schumer have always suffered from the peculiar malady of wanting to crack down on inanimate objects (guns) instead of criminals, and of criminalizing people who have done nothing wrong. In 1969, New York City residents who owned long guns for decades were ordered to come forward to register their guns. Assured by the City that this action was not intended for eventual confiscation, law-abiding gun owners obeyed this tyrannical directive. People who had never broken the law were told 22 years later that if they did not turn in their weapons, they would be guilty of a crime.

Thus, an entire slew of honest people was transformed into law-breakers that could now be cracked down on, giving Chuck Schumer and other gun grabbers the illusion that their gun control measures are fighting crime. Real criminals are laughing—and are applauding the ascendancy of Senator Chuck Schumer.

Blackmun: Death of a Despot

As expected, the death of retired Supreme Court Justice Harry Blackmun last week was met with the usual accolades reserved for those who impose their personal will in a non-democratic, tyrannical manner. Tributes in the *New York Times* and other media expounded on how Blackmun "grew in office" while on his "personal journey" from conservative to liberal jurist, becoming a champion of the "poor and disenfranchised."

It is axiomatic that a public figure only "grows" in office when he becomes more liberal. Indeed, Blackmun was the 20th Century embodiment of the judge as despot, overruling through judicial fiat the voice of the majority, and becoming the single most identifiable representative of a judiciary gone mad. Yes, Harry Blackmun "grew" all right, just as Al Capone also "grew."

Best remembered as the author of the notorious *Roe v. Wade* decision that struck down all abortion restrictions in the fifty states, Blackmun's view was that states had no independent authority, the will of the people and of elected representatives didn't matter, and dictator judges should rule over all aspects of American life. To hell with the voters, majority view and the consent of the governed. Harry Blackmun knew best.

Blackmun found unenumerated "penumbras" and "rights" in the Constitution which were mischievously hiding for 200 years until he came to the rescue and discovered them. His pernicious decisions flouted the public will at every conceivable turn. Though the country overwhelmingly favored capital punishment, and the Constitution explicitly permits it, Blackmun "grew" to oppose the death penalty, and imposed his personal view on an unwilling majority. "From this day forward, I no longer shall tinker with the machinery of death," he said with condescending profundity.

He found "rights" where none existed — such as homosexual "rights" — and denied voters the power of law enacted democratically through their elected officials. All of these issues — abortion, homosexual rights, capital punishment, law enforcement policies — are legitimate public topics that ought to be scrutinized and debated through the long, painful and sometimes tedious mechanisms of representative government and democracy. But Blackmun and his cohorts usurped democratic processes. As his partner in crime, Justice William Brennan once said, "With five votes around here you can do anything."

Democracy is a very tenuous and unlikely development, given the self-centered nature of man. The precarious system of three dueling branches of government acting as checks on each other was deliberately created by the Founders in order to make the legislative process more difficult, under the theory that most laws take away personal freedoms. Against the Founders' intentions and against any explicit language in the Constitution, the Supreme Court has become the final arbiter of law.

Thomas Jefferson understood that if any branch of government captured this power exclusively, it would soon rule the country like a tyrant. He said, "Whoever hath an absolute authority to interpret any written or spoken laws, it is He who is truly the Lawgiver to all intents and purposes, and not the person who first wrote or spoke them."

By arrogating to itself the power to interpret the Constitution, the Supreme Court has effectively grabbed power on every important national problem. Only the arduous and difficult amendment process and the impeachment of judges can rein in the judicial power grab run amok.

No democratically elected legislature would ever have passed an equivalent of the Miranda law, which requires police to tell criminals that they need not confess. Likewise, no legislature would have enacted forced busing. But the courts, not answerable to the people, flout the consent of the voters. Since the 1950's, it has been the practice of liberals, when they do not like the majority opinion, to go to the courts to work their treachery.

The concept of "judicial review," which is a court's inquiry into the constitutionality of law, assumes the courts know better than elected officials and the people. However, the judicial system is merely supposed to mete out justice to individuals (parties to a case), not strike down laws. Defenders of this kind of judicial encroachment claim that the courts are defending the rights of the minority. But this assumes that the majority's rapaciousness must always be checked by guardians unelected to their positions. If this concept is not inimical to democracy, what is?

The most important check on the majority is that there is seldom a *permanent* majority in a true representative democracy. There are natural restraints against majority tyranny since today's winners may be tomorrow's losers. But the tyranny of Harry Blackmun and the Supreme Court knew no bounds. Unlike legislatures, judges are not inclined to compromise, making their laws the least democratic of all.

Americans appear helpless to rise up against the actions of the Supreme Court. But that need not be the case. Jefferson thought states had the right to ignore federal laws their legislatures found unconstitutional. Teddy Roosevelt believed every time the Supreme

Court struck down a law or discovered a new "right," the question should be voted on during the next national election. A perfect test case for this would be California's Proposition 187, which the majority of voters endorsed, and which denied tax dollars to illegal aliens, but which was struck down by a federal judge.

The legacy of Harry Blackmun, who did indeed "grow" in office, is a government based on force and not on consent, which, as Jefferson said, is "a government of wolves over sheep."

Dinkins: Still a Loser

David Dinkins — degenerate socialist and cultural heathen — is back in the news. Six years since being tossed from office after presiding over the most failed mayoralty in the history of New York City, the former mayor has shown how little he has grown. As the most prominent person arrested at the Amadou Diallo circus, Dinkins performed this display of public service ten years too late. The better New York would have been had Dinkins been locked up his first day in office.

It is difficult to think of one particular word or expression that could accurately summarize the Dinkins years. During that horrible era, in which the very name of New York became synonymous with rampant street crime and the collapse of the once-greatest city in the world, the number of murders and crimes of violence was so high that New York became known as "Fear City."

With a record of so complete and abject failure, the kindest word to describe the Dinkins years might be "amazing." Amazing, in the same sense that Casey Stengel referred to his 1962 New York Mets, in that they were so amazingly bad. Indeed, recalling the Dinkins mayoralty is akin to remembering the bubonic plague. Take a stroll down memory sewer.

Perhaps more than any other event, the riots in Crown Heights, Brooklyn became the defining moment of the Dinkins tenure. It said as much about the man as it said about the state of the city. In 1991, after a car driven by a Hasidic Jew accidentally killed a seven year old black boy named Gavin Cato, black savages ran wild for three days—unchallenged and uninterrupted—while Dinkins and Police Commissioner Lee Brown fiddled. The marauding rioters eventually spotted Yankel Rosenbaum, an Australian Torah student, and chanting "Get the Jew," Rosenbaum was stabbed to death. Before dying, Rosenbaum identified his killer as Lemrick Nelson, who was found with the bloody knife. An all-black jury subsequently acquitted Nelson and went out to celebrate with him.

The lawlessness of the Dinkins years was also typified by the boycott of a Korean grocery store. After some black militants claimed that the store owners mistreated a black customer whom the owners suspected of shoplifting, they organized an illegal boycott, defying a court order by refusing to stay a certain distance away from the store, and attempting to put the Koreans out of business. Day after day, the boycotters disregarded the law and threatened and intimidated any customers who wanted to patronize the store. Dinkins refused to have police enforce the law, allowing the illegal harassment to continue for months. Former Mayor Ed Koch called the boycotters "urban terrorists."

In one of the greatest acts of tyranny in New York's history, Dinkins pushed through legislation in 1991 which effectively banned many types of semi-automatic rifles. What he did, in effect, was criminalize honest gun owners who had owned these weapons for upwards of 20 to 30 years and had never committed a crime. These people were simply expected to turn their rifles in without a fight. The bill was so awful and unreasonable that even liberal Democrats on the City Council's Public Safety Committee questioned Dinkins forcefully on certain aspects of the bill at the committee hearing.

One of the more memorable moments of the public hearing (which was packed with law-abiding gun owners) occurred when Committee Chairman Sheldon Leffler asked Dinkins how he expected to enforce such a law. Dinkins replied, "We will enforce this law the same way we enforce every other law."

As the Manhattan-based *Federation Eagle* reported at the time, "The resounding laughter in the chamber was so loud and heartfelt that even committee members joined in, betraying smiles and snickers at the mayor's stupidity."

The logic behind Dinkins' legislation and the feeble thought processes of his own mind concluded that he could not and would not do anything about real violent criminals, so he intended to crack down hard on the law-abiding.

In one of the most tragic episodes of the Dinkins years, Brian Watkins, a 22 year old tourist from Utah, was stabbed to death while coming to the aid of his mother during a mugging attempt on the subway. The incident sent shockwaves throughout the nation as typifying New York as the crime capital of the world. Even in the midst of this tragedy, Dinkins could not help but make an ass of himself. He stated that the incident, a stabbing with a knife, demonstrated the need for more *gun* control.

In the year leading up to his defeat, the *Federation Eagle* ran a monthly feature called the "Dinkinsism of the Month," presenting the mayor's most asinine and ridiculous statements. At a press conference just before the 1992 Democratic Convention at Madison Square Garden, reporters questioned Dinkins about the odd choice of New York for the convention, given the city's astronomical crime rate. Dinkins replied, "To suggest that New York City is riddled with crime is just plain inaccurate."

The Associated Press reported that 32 conventioneers actually rented bullet proof vests from a vest-mobile traveling around Madison Square Garden. Not even the President of the City Council was safe. His baby-sitter and two children were taken hostage by an armed bandit. Make no mistake, New York was terrified.

Other Dinkinsisms included, "I will be the toughest mayor on crime this city has ever seen." And, "After the Rodney King verdict in Los Angeles we worked to control things here — using some of the things we learned in Crown Heights, I would add."

When a known Washington Heights drug dealer was shot and killed by police in self-defense, Dinkins used taxpayers' money to pay for the hoodlum's funeral and to fly his family from the Dominican Republic. Rather than stand with the police, Dinkins met in sympathy with the drug dealer's family.

In a Greenwich Village park, Dinkins unveiled two statues paid for with tax dollars — one of two homosexuals on a park bench with their arms around each other; the other of two lesbians holding hands. He called this "great progress."

When Dinkins was handcuffed and arrested the other day, he did more for New York in five short minutes than he had done as mayor during four long years.

Culbert a Victim of the Thought Police

Another heretic has been burned at the stake. Joseph Culbert, police captain turned scapegoat, has been sacrificed at the altar of political correctness for acts of perfidy. The alleged treachery for which Culbert has been stoned is a thought crime, a violation of the new orthodoxy, a perceived insensitivity on a matter concerning race. No greater transgression can a public person commit, and the Thought Police have once again exacted an awful retribution. Throw him to the lions.

The genesis of this sordid tale begins, ironically, with the funeral of Patrick Dorismond, the black man shot to death by New York City police after a scuffle, the details of which are still unclear. Nevertheless, the Dorismond case — on the heels of the acquittals in the Amadou Diallo trial — has provided cop-hating zealots with yet another opportunity to spew their poison in front of television cameras. It was for that reason, to combat potential riots, that Culbert, the commander of the 104th Precinct in Queens, was even present at the funeral. What happened in the immediate aftermath is yet not completely known, but a stubbornly consistent version of events has emerged.

Apparently, according to events described by four independent sources (including one who has heard the tape), Culbert was returning from the Dorismond funeral in a car with two other policemen. He placed a call to his boss, Deputy Chief Dewey Fong, as a routine update. Having left a message on Fong's answering machine, Culbert believed he had hung up the phone but had not, allowing the subsequent conversation in the car to be picked up on Fong's answering machine. At that point, one of the officers relayed a story — which is surprisingly well-known amongst police in Queens — that Fong had once entered a police station wearing white street clothes and holding a paper bag. Not recognizing the Chinese-American Fong, the officer at the desk called out, inquiring whether anyone at the station had ordered Chinese food — mistaking the Chief for a delivery man. The cop in the car, having concluded the anecdote, then broke out into a raucous laugh.

Now, anyone who doesn't think this story is funny is either lying or has no sense of humor. Visualizing Fong listening to this on his answering machine is yet a further scream.

Culbert, for his part, was silent in the car. Fong, upon hearing the tape, filed a discrimination and harassment complaint against Culbert to the NYPD's Equal Employment Opportunity office, resulting in the captain's transfer out of his precinct after only two and a half months on the job.

When the story broke, disinformation appeared to be the order of the day. The news across New York City was that Culbert had made a "racial slur" against Fong. Evidence, however, was strangely lacking and, even if it existed, was curiously suppressed. It appears obvious that the crackdown on thought crimes and thought speech are flourishing. If Culbert didn't say anything, what did he do?

Well, perhaps the Thought Police believe he should have reprimanded the officer for the crime of imparting a hilarious story which might have rubbed Fong the wrong way. Or maybe Culbert — perish the thought — actually agreed that the story was funny. In any event, Culbert has been punished for the perception that he has violated political correctness, despite community civic organizations' support of his crime-fighting efforts.

As for Fong (who has not returned calls for comment), he has, according to police sources, shown himself to be a small man with a huge racial chip on his shoulder. One source described him as an "affirmative action" hire who has used his race to advance in the department. Fong was originally denied entry into the NYPD because of his height. When the statute was changed, he sued the department, claiming he would have been promoted faster had the height requirement not delayed him in the first place.

According to Bob Holden, President of the Juniper Park Civic Association, Fong's superiority complex was responsible for the removal of an officer in the Queens community affairs division, Linda Marmara, because she "made him wait" once in a car. Fong is a very impatient man. Holden also spoke to Fong's boss, Chief James Tuller. Holden said, "He [Tuller] was clear that Culbert made no racial remark on the tape." Holden has since organized a community protest in support of Culbert, demanding his reinstatement to his precinct. By itself, this is an earth-shattering development, given the usual cowardice that public persons display when a heretic is lynched for perceived racial thought crimes. Most Queens politicians, conversely, have been predictably silent on Culbert's behalf.

What will become of Culbert is unclear, but it is an experience he undoubtedly will never forget. The unforgiving forces of intolerance, with their speech codes, demands of adherence to cultural orthodoxy — forcing citizens to suppress their freedom — and mind control, have claimed another casualty. In Queens, Joseph Culbert, sold out by the NYPD brass to appease the fringe radicals, is the latest victim of the Thought Police, always searching for pagans, ruining careers and making automaton conformists out of free-thinking men.

Until We Meet Again, Jamie

The following remarks were spoken in eulogy at the funeral service for 11 year old Jamie Noelle Kocher at the United Methodist Church in Glendale, Queens. This book is dedicated to her.

Dying was the only thing Jamie ever did that was out of character.

So filled with exuberance and spirit, she was the most energetic child I've ever seen, especially given the scourge that was afflicting her. Sharper than ever throughout her protracted ordeal and the pain she endured, her wit, charm and determination never let up for a minute.

On behalf of the School Board, I'd like to say that we're very proud of Jamie in District 24. We have 27 schools and 36,000 students in our district encompassing a large section of Queens and we are very proud indeed of the example Jamie set, always showing her courage, her determination and her feistiness. This was an example not only for her classmates and the other children in our district, but for all of us.

I'd also like to acknowledge Ken Lombardi, Jamie's principal at our school PS 91, who was always there for her, caring for her throughout the difficult times at school. And also Jamie's teacher, Donna Franquinha, and the entire family of PS 91 for their extraordinary efforts on Jamie's behalf and the caring and love they showed her. They are the ones who were with her every day and who really deserve the credit. We are very proud of all of them.

When I speak of Jamie, I think I can speak for the people like me, who met Jamie after she was already ill. It is remarkable the impression that she made in the face of such pain. She was never lacking for fun and sharing wonderful times. Often, it's not the *length* of time you know someone, but the intensity of the relationship and how well you know the person. When Jamie and I first met, I felt an obligation to her certainly as one of my students. And also as a child from my community. But it was always more than that. I remember being devastated by the unfairness of her affliction and my obligation to do whatever was humanly possibly to save her from a situation that I will never truly understand and that I will never be able to reconcile.

I've been emotionally distraught before and distressed over injustices, but Jamie's plight was the first time something like this had ever affected me physically. My pain was unbearable at times, made better only by being with Jamie and sharing happy times with her.

When I went around the community speaking on Jamie's behalf to local groups, raising money for the Jamie Fund or asking for donations of blood and platelets, I saw a uniting and outpouring of love on the part of this community like I had never seen before. I was overwhelmed. I remember when I spoke at a community board meeting when Jamie was on the brink, going through another experimental treatment. It was unsure if she would survive another week. People were donating out of their pockets and groups were donating raffle money. A month later, the president of the hockey league presented a check for over $1,000 to the Jamie Fund. And this was at a meeting where Jamie showed up like a conquering hero to say, "Thank you!"

Jamie certainly brought out the best in people. That's why she was named "Person of the Year" by the Glendale Register. I'd also like to acknowledge Walter Sanchez, the publisher of the Glendale Register, for all of the coverage he gave to Jamie throughout her entire ordeal.

Being in media myself, I don't like it very much when anyone gets more press than me, but Jamie had us all beat. Darryl Strawberry had gotten sick around the same time as Jamie. What other 55 pound child could knock a six-foot five-inch star baseball player out of the headlines! But leave it to Jamie to get the attention of stars like Chuck Norris and Magic Johnson, who became her good friends.

I've heard a lot about Jamie's truthfulness and bluntness, qualities I admire very much. But she was also a bit of a wise guy, very sarcastic indeed. One time we were playing a game after having dinner and I kept calling her "Wamie," speaking to her like a baby. This annoyed her to no end. Naturally, that was all the more reason to keep doing it. Her little brother Michael thought it was hilarious, so he started laughing and saying it too. "Wamie, Wamie." This absolutely drove her crazy. "Alright," she said to me. "If you keep calling me that I'm not speaking to you." I replied, "Fine, so don't speak to me." She then said, "Anyway, why should I speak to a grown man who wears his hair down to his shoulders?"

She thought she had me at that point. I immediately shot back, "Well, what about your hero, the country singer Billy Ray Cyrus? (Jamie had a nice picture taken with him.) He wears his hair down to his shoulders." She responded, "Yeah, but at least *he's* cute."

I hope this was not one of Jamie's moments of truthfulness.

You know, it wasn't easy growing up Catholic, what with all the strange things we were taught in Catholic school. And Pastor Stevens, I'd appreciate it if you didn't tell my Monsignor what I'm saying here. First, there's Catholic guilt. We were always made to feel guilty about everything. Also, the girls were warned to never wear patent leather shoes, because the boys would look at them to see the reflection up their skirts. I don't think this works, although I keep trying.

But the one thing that we did learn that I have always believed was that this life is not the end, that we would be with the people we love again. It is the Faith in this that sustains us.

Lately, Jamie and I were in the habit of exchanging e-mails. Last week I sent her the message, "I love you, Jamie." She wrote back, "I love you, too." I was going to visit her last weekend, but on Friday she wrote to tell me she was going upstate for the weekend. I wrote back saying I'd visit her next week when she got back. But as it turned out, she was too sick to go. Then on Tuesday morning I got the call that Jamie had left us. Tuesday was one of the worst days of my life.

I wanted to tell her one more thing, but I know that she already knows. I have dedicated my fourth book, titled, "Don't Take It Personally," to my inspiration, Jamie Kocher, who I used to lift in the air with one hand because she was so light.

And so my beloved friend, Jamie—"Wamie"—until we meet again, rest in peace.

VI
IMMIGRATION

The Coming Dark Age

Most Americans, sadly, are totally unaware of the radical racial transformation that their country is undergoing. Because civilizations are never destructed in one night, the slow and incremental change in the United States remains an oblivious occurrence to many. The best example is that of a frog in boiling water. Toss the frog in the scalding pot and he'll jump right out. But place the frog in room temperature water and heat it up slowly, degree by degree, and he'll never realize a thing. Soon, he'll be cooked.

According to the Census Bureau, the same thing is happening to the white majority in the United States. Because such a transformation is gradual, and often unnoticed from day to day, Americans are allowing their own dispossession without a whimper. By the time they realize what has happened it may be too late.

In 1953, East Berliners were protesting madly against the Soviet-imposed communist regime. The Communists maintained that their dictatorship was justified, as in the people's best interest. In a sarcastic remark that has gone down as a classic, the playwright Bertolt Brecht remarked, "Wouldn't it be simpler in that case if the Government dissolved the people and elected another?" Such is the disdain with which the American government holds its people, allowing policies which Americans undoubtedly would oppose if they focused on the consequences.

But it cannot be fairly said that the information is not out there, merely that Americans have not absorbed what is actually happening. In fact, the fresh data released by the Census Bureau is stark, startling and horrifying. What is happening to the composition of the American populace can only be characterized as the single most radical transformation of a people in the history of the world.

The 2000 Census counted 281.4 million Americans, a 13.1 percent increase over the 1990 total of 248.7 million. In 1990 whites were still 75 percent of the population (which was down from the 90 percent of 1960.) Today, whites have slipped to just 69.1 percent of the population, a seven point loss in only ten years.

For the first time ever, Hispanics now outnumber blacks as a total of U.S. population, 12.5 to 12.3 percent. Asians (3.5 percent) and a mix of others account for the rest. All of these increases by non-white groups come, of course, at the expense of whites. And while the numbers are disturbing in and of themselves, the true catastrophe lies in the trends — the racial projections for the coming century, which can justifiably be called the New Dark Age.

According to the Census Bureau, if current trends in immigration and birthrates continue, whites will drop to under 50 percent of the population by the year 2060. Therefore, the descendants of the founding civilization of the United States will have voluntarily handed over to alien civilizations an America transformed. This will be the first time in history that a people will have been displaced without a shot being fired.

Blacks by 2060 will increase slightly to 13.3 percent. Hispanics would balloon to 26.6 percent and Asians to 9.8 percent. Hispanics, therefore, a group historically occupying a low single-digit percentage of the U.S. population, will comprise more than one-quarter of the United States!

At that point, the entire American population is projected to be more than 432 million, which would be the equivalent of adding to today's America the entire population of the United States in 1945 — 145 million people. This is a figure which may be unsupportable economically and environmentally even if all the newcomers were white and English-speaking. But they will not be. Virtually all will be third world. At that point, the geographic break-up or partition of the United States may be the only salvation as maintaining a semblance of Western Civilization and white hegemony.

But the numbers are even worse than they appear because the Census Bureau does not fully take into account the impact of illegal immigration. The Bureau estimates illegals currently in the United States to be six million (double what they estimated in 1993.) But researchers at Northeastern University in Boston estimate the number at closer to 13 million, which will hasten the day of white displacement.

The problem, however, is not only illegal immigration and high non-white birthrates. The problem is *legal* immigration, which is not only 90 percent non-white, but is at soaring, unmanageable levels. The legal immigration population is growing at 700,000 to 900,000 a year, meaning one out of ten Americans is foreign-born. Current levels of alien entry, moreover, are well above historical levels.

Whites, on a certain level, understand the unpleasantness of racial change. The Census Bureau reports that "white flight" is more alive than ever, as whites increasingly move away from non-white, immigrant-heavy locales. Some whites may say they like third world immigration, but the stark numbers reveal that very few actually want to live amongst them. White are overwhelmingly moving to suburbs and other white enclaves, even within cities. And whites are now a majority in only 52 of America's 100 largest cities, down from 70 only a decade ago.

The only encouraging thing about this impending disaster, this coming dissolution of the United States, is that it is a result of politics and government policy. It is not a natural, inevitable phenomenon. It doesn't have to happen. In other words, *it can be changed and averted* if only Americans rise up against their elitist unresponsive government — before it's too late.

"Wretched Refuse" a Health Hazard

At the peak of the first great wave of immigration in 1910, as much as 15 percent of the 24,000 immigrants refused admission to the United States were turned away because they were carriers of contagious diseases. Notwithstanding the historical myth of "open borders" during that period, all arrivals at Ellis Island were rigorously inspected by teams of doctors.

Part of this procedure was informed by the memory of the return of cholera and smallpox with the Irish immigrants of the

1840's. It was also rationalized by plain common sense — a factor conspicuously absent from today's disastrous immigration policies. With two to three million aliens entering the United States illegally every year, the country has never found itself so dangerously unprotected against immigration's impact on current public health.

Aliens appear to be very well informed as to the cowardice that defines America's laws of lunacy. An inordinate number of sick aliens are trekking to the United States for free medical treatment, just as a great number come for welfare. Since state and federal laws do not permit public hospitals to turn away patients, so-called "medical immigrants" are taking taxis straight from the airport to the emergency room.

The hardest hit locales are the big cities like New York and Chicago, which are being flooded with aliens who have advanced cases of leprosy, cancer and AIDS. The exact number can never be known because aliens often lie about why they are here. In addition, doctors frequently refuse to collect data that may encourage anti-immigrant sentiment. Lewis Goldfrank, the director of emergency services at Bellevue Hospital Center in Manhattan, does not distinguish between sick patients. "Should I wonder whether this is the guy from Third Avenue who doesn't have any money or the guy from the Third World who doesn't have any? That's not my job," he says. "I'm a doctor."

While at first glance this may seem to be the humane attitude of someone who has taken the Hippocratic Oath, there are serious public health considerations in ignoring alien and disease presence in the United States. Certainly, the government should not be allowing these people in in the first place, but Dr. Goldfrank's attitude will not only give him more sick aliens at Bellevue's doorstep, it also aids in creating a more dangerous disease-filled environment for Americans — not to mention a steep financial burden.

Last year, Dr. Goldfrank treated a West African with kidney failure who had tried to get dialysis in Guinea. At the Guinea hospital where he could not get care, he saw a notice on the hospital bulletin board informing that if he could somehow get to Paris or New York, he could get free dialysis. In February 1988, he walked into the

Bellevue emergency room with fatal levels of potassium in his blood and Medicaid has been paying for weekly dialysis ever since. This for someone who has never paid a dime into the system or in American taxes. Wonderful news for Americans who fought in wars, paid taxes all their lives, and find themselves on a waiting list.

On a typical day in 1998, the admitted patient population at Bellevue was 701 patients — 160 not American citizens and 70 ineligible for government assistance, sure indications they were illegal aliens. Bellevue had to treat them anyway. In 1997, New York City hospitals spent $1.2 billion on patients who could not or would not pay. These are also invariably illegals.

Jackson Memorial Hospital in Florida maintains a much tougher policy on aliens. Staff will stabilize a life-threatening condition in the emergency room, but will not admit indigents who cannot prove legal residency. They will notify the Immigration and Naturalization Service if a patient is illegal. They also often find that it is more cost-efficient to pay for return airfare than to treat a disease. A spokeswoman for Jackson Memorial, Maria Rosa Gonzalez, states, "Our first responsibility is to the people of Miami-Dade County. And we're not ashamed to admit it."

But more than costs, the "wretched refuse" arriving on our teeming shores are reigniting deadly diseases in the United States that were long thought extinct. Tuberculosis, believed eradicated by the 1970's, is surging in certain parts of the country, thanks to immigration from regions like Latin America, where the disease is endemic. Of 6,000 patients afflicted with leprosy, 90 percent were refugees or aliens from Southeast Asia or Mexico.

Likewise, measles is flaring up in Hispanic areas, particularly among recent arrivals from Latin America. Cholera, malaria and dengue fever have also been reported in the United States recently. The U.S. Institute of Medicine has predicted "with some confidence" that if the incurable mosquito-borne disease, yellow fever, returns from Africa and Amazonia, public health defenses could become overwhelmed. It stated, "100,000 would become ill... and 10,000 would die within 90 days."

American lawmakers, for purely political reasons, have ignored the unseemly cultural and economic consequences resulting from America's disastrous immigration policies. But the health scourge brought on by the presence of aliens may finally force them to act.

Reconquista

The term "Hispanic" does not, by definition, specifically identify a person by race. In a technical sense, there is no "Hispanic" race. It is purely a cultural constraint.

Invented in 1977 by the Office of Management and Budget in order for Hispanics to take part more effectively in the welfare spoils system, the designation "Hispanic" was defined as "a person of Mexican, Puerto Rican, Cuban, Central or South American, or other Spanish culture or origin, regardless of race." "Hispanics" can, therefore, be white (like Fidel Castro and Desi Arnaz, both Cubans) or black (like Sammy Sosa, a Dominican.)

Nevertheless, Hispanic activists, who for decades insisted they were white because of the accompanying advantages, began lobbying the federal government to recognize them as non-white when there appeared to be more money in that designation. In reality, most Hispanics are mestizos, a mixture of the races, with Indian blood being the most prevalent.

The organizations that represent Hispanic interests are vociferously anti-white and anti-American, even utilizing the term "La Raza" (the race) as a synonym for Hispanics. It would be startling to most Americans to realize that there are organizations, funded in part by tax dollars and in part by foundations, that have as their ultimate goal the "reconquest" of parts of the United States in order to form a new nation, "Aztlan" (brown continent.) This goal is described by Hispanic subversives as "Reconquista."

The four main organizations that speak for Hispanic interests are the League of United Latin American Citizens (LULAC), the

Mexican American Legal Defense and Education Fund (MALDEF), the National Council of La Raza (La Raza), and the Movimiento Estudiantil Chicano de Aztlan (MECha). These groups differ in certain technical respects and in some of their methods. Their means of support and sustenance also vary, but their primary objectives are all the same.

If the aims of these groups were to be summed up in one general mission statement, their goal would be to subvert the will of the American majority, obliterate historical American culture and overthrow any remnants of the European founding, settlement and heritage of the United States. Not only are these groups at odds with the wishes of the average American, they are most fanatical and determined on the very points on which they are *most* at odds. In fact, it is clear that these groups exist precisely because of these conflicts.

All these radical entities support continued massive Hispanic immigration to the United States in order to bolster their numbers -- basically an America without borders. They want total and unconditional amnesty for illegal aliens and a complete halt to deportation of illegals. They fight relentlessly for any tax-funded government benefits for all non-citizens, whether they are here legally or not. They favor securing all the rights reserved exclusively for American citizens, including the right to vote in American elections, to non-citizens. American citizenship, therefore, would be rendered meaningless.

These groups all demand official recognition of Hispanic culture, language and national holidays, as well as the necessary funds to finance their promotion. This would include street names, public monuments and official observances to commemorate Hispanic history and heroes. They want all government services in Spanish, including public school instruction.

Spanish would be recognized by government as co-equal with English, and Spanish would be the only official language in locales which are predominantly Hispanic. Affirmative action would spread to the utmost benefit of Hispanics. Essentially, these groups are demanding the very conditions that would exist if Mexico's army were to invade and conquer the United States.

LULAC opposes the military defense of the Mexican border -- even to stop drug smuggling -- because they "might easily violate the civil rights of those they intervene with." MALDEF, which exists primarily through the generosity of the Ford Foundation, is the group responsible for bilingual education in public schools, having supported the plaintiffs in *Lau v. Nichols*, and securing free public education for illegal aliens through *Plyer v. Doe* in 1982. Mario Obledo, a MALDEF official, has said, "California is going to be a Hispanic state. Anyone who does not like it should leave."

These Hispanic groups don't appear particularly worried about their ability to accomplish their ends. They believe that through sheer numbers, they will be able to accomplish the reconquest they seek. Comprising just under 12 percent of the American population, they are on the verge of overtaking blacks as America's largest minority. If current immigration and birthrates continue, Hispanics will go from 32 million to 98 million in 50 years. If that day arrives, the "reconquista" is complete and the American nation no longer exists, the white minority will curse today's politicians who allowed it to happen.

Cardinal Sins On Immigration

The hierarchy of the Catholic Church, when it addresses areas outside the realm of doctrine and veers into social admonitions, tends to wander into left field. Far left field.

Whether the issue is welfare, the redistribution of wealth, socialist unionism or the death penalty, America's bishops and cardinals serendipitously arrive at the most liberal position on all these matters. Even Pope John Paul II, the alleged Stonewall Jackson of so-called traditional Catholic teaching and indeed a pillar of unyielding moral strength who played an indispensable role in the destruction of communism, has issued some very peculiar economic statements which can charitably be described as socialist.

The exception to this distressingly pronounced liberalism is assumed to be on the issue of abortion. But even there the bishops have come under criticism from conservatives. At the just-concluded annual conference of America's 250 Catholic bishops, the clergy refused to threaten excommunication to Catholic politicians who support abortion. Moreover, there hasn't been a memorable sermon from the pulpit on sin, hell or damnation in years.

But it is on immigration that Catholic leadership is most confused and most convoluted. Last week, Cardinal John O'Connor of New York proposed that illegal aliens from Central America be permitted to make a "round-trip" visit to their families in their hurricane-ravaged homelands. He said, "Would it be absurd to suggest that there be some kind of validation of their status, that they be permitted to go down and visit their suffering families in the Central American countries so badly hit by the hurricane?"

Yes, it would.

Here is a churchman advocating that people who have broken American laws be rewarded instead of deported. Furthermore, O'Connor wants a "validation" of status. In other words, break the law, take a leave to attend to personal business, and then the government will accommodate in an official manner your continuance of breaking the law.

O'Connor continued, "They [illegal aliens] do the most menial work, but much of the money that they make goes to those who are even more impoverished in Central America." Again, this is a statement of support for illegal activities, with the added twist that— lamentably, in O'Connor's view — the poor law-breakers are not benefiting *enough* from their law-breaking.

Liberalism has always defined compassion in the most odd manner—usually as taking other people's money through force and coercion to use for the benefit of those who did not earn it. Thus, the Church's outlandish support of every government-sponsored social program which taxpayers are forced to subsidize whether they like it or not. True compassion, of course, is voluntary.

On immigration, the open borders sentiment of the Church is at odds with the law and the democratic will of the American people. But the Church does not merely advocate the changing of the law, they support those who *break* the law.

John Paul II has frequently instructed Western nations that they have a moral obligation to take in all immigrants who want to enter. The West must share the wealth with those who haven't the capacity to create it themselves. Such admonitions are silly and misguided. Again, if these clerics had their way, American citizens would be forced to give their earnings — and their country — away through coercion.

These nonsensical views are not solely the province of the Catholic Church. Other Christian denominations have joined in the chorus. Pat Robertson supports more immigration from south of the border, claiming these people support "family values" and are "our kind of voters." Has he lost his grip on reality? The most profound result of these newcomers has been a dilution of American culture and the gradual formation of what Hispanic activists call "Aztlan" (Bronze Continent) which would displace the United States. Ralph Reed and Billy Graham have also expressed support for more non-white immigration. Rev. Graham says Americans must take aliens into our hearts, homes, and "into our marriages." And these are so-called "conservative" Christians.

What possesses these men to spout such blather? Interestingly, self-identified Christians have been identified in poll after poll as being strongly opposed to current mass immigration. The clergy, on the other hand, are probably affected by certain scripture passages. Leviticus 19:33-34 states, "If a stranger sojourn with thee in your land, ye shall not vex him. But the stranger that dwelleth with you shall be unto you as one born among you, and thou shalt love him as thyself."

Because of Matthew 25:31-46, when Jesus states, "I was a stranger and ye took me not in..." clergy often suggest that anyone prevented from entering the United States might be, well, Jesus. Peter Brimelow writes, "The problem, however, is this: there are rather a lot of Jesuses out there. No conceivable U.S. immigration policy can 'minister' to all of them."

A more realistic passage as applied to the American plight might be from essayist Michael Masters, who wrote, "Unless we adopt moral beliefs in keeping with the realities of today's demographics, we will not survive the mounting wave of Third World immigration, procreation and miscegenation."

Indeed, it is so much nonsense that Americans have a moral obligation to accommodate foreigners, much less so in the case of aliens who strive to supplant our country and our culture.

Immigration Policy Proves Deadly

About a decade ago, an Israeli general was asked by an American journalist about the extreme nature of some of Israel's security and anti-terrorism policies, despite often widespread criticism of their implementation. Why, the questioner inquired, did Israel ignore the political considerations in forming its plans? "Because," the general responded, "unlike the United States, Israel actually has to take the prospect of war seriously."

This response, in its profound clarity, explains the reckless irresponsibility of American politicians' propensity to place politics above American domestic security considerations. In their endless desire to pander fecklessly to radical internal elements, American lawmakers have ignored disastrous immigration laws which have allowed virtually any human timebomb to walk through unprotected borders.

Ignoring the will of across-the-board American public opinion against increased levels of immigration and, in fact, in favor of drastically reduced levels, the American immigration policymakers created a disaster -- and then allowed it to stand. Now, 3,000 dead bodies lie somewhere in the downtown New York rubble as the cursed monument to this policy. Indeed, no one in his right mind could possibly support American immigration laws. But the political considerations were too great, and America has paid an unspeakable price. Maybe now America will take the prospect of war "seriously."

Now, it seems, everything is on the table. Because of the World Trade Center attack, all policies -- airport security, covert military operations, and immigration -- are subject to a new look. Even racial profiling is attempting a comeback into respectability.

So how exactly could these foreign terrorists waltz into the United States and live comfortably without scrutiny for months and years, all the while plotting to hijack planes to kill Americans and topple buildings?

In fact, the cities of Jersey City and Passaic in northern New Jersey, with a full view of the World Trade Center, are so teeming with aliens that the killers were able to blend in unnoticed, using American stupidity to their full advantage. This was not simply a case of taking advantage of the benefits of an open society. That part of the plot only applies *after having already entered the country*. No, it is the part which allowed them to enter in the first place which is so unforgivable.

Thirteen men arrested by federal authorities for involvement in the attack lived in northern New Jersey, in the same neighborhoods where the 1993 WTC suspects also resided. Peter Woolsey, a terrorism expert from Farleigh Dickinson University said, "You have easy transportation and you have a rip-roaring economy where you can get a job and present yourself as a normal immigrant working to save a little money. It's a good place to cover your tracks and wait until you're told to act. In the meantime, you need to occupy yourself. Once you get a job and a bank account set up, you have a sense of legitimacy."

Oh, how convenient. These squalid criminals, with no legitimate reason for entering the United States, set up shop, join gyms, get jobs, open bank accounts, and buy airline tickets in their own names. American immigration policy does not discriminate in favor of skilled persons with something to offer, does not enforce an English proficiency requirement and does not, God forbid, take culture or race into account. This is the policy that brought down the towers.

The border with Mexico is totally unprotected. The Border Patrol is overworked and undermanned. Aliens walk through without resistance. Persons with visas enter the United States and then disappear. No one keeps track of them. Family reunification policy guides immigration laws, allowing women to cross the border illegally, give birth to an American citizen, and traipse the rest of the family through. Uncontrolled borders have the rest of the world laughing at the United States and the terrorists are having the biggest laugh. Many of the suspects now apprehended were actually picked up because of immigration violations, which only serves to demonstrate the ease with which aliens can flaunt the laws when they want to.

There are approximately six to eight million Moslems living in the United States today, compared to only 100,000 in 1960. There are roughly 3.5 million Arabs. In the two weeks since the attack, American officials have gone to pains to stress that Islam is a religion of peace and that most American Moslems condemn the attacks. Nevertheless, even peace-loving American Moslems and Arabs have got to question an immigration policy that is so porous that even overt America-haters are allowed in.

According to a *Los Angeles Times* op-ed entitled, "It Matters What Kind of Islam Prevails," some Moslems living in the United States do advocate a violent overthrow of the American government in favor of a theocratic Islamic state. Writer Daniel Pipes states, "In the words of a teacher at the Al-Ghazly Islamic School in Jersey City, N.J., 'Our short-term goal is to introduce Islam. In the long term, we must save American society. Allah will ask why I did not speak about Islam, because this piece of land is Allah's property.'"

Pipes continued, "Some of this ilk even talk about overthrowing the U.S. government and replacing it with an Islamic one. Although it sounds bizarre, this attitude attracts serious and widespread support among Muslims."

Pipes' editorial was written in July of 1999 and fell on deaf ears. Maybe the sounds of Americans crying will finally force another look at an immigration policy that is absurd, unsound and now, deadly.

U.S. Law Welcomes Terrorists

Americans are largely ignorant of many of the outrageous specifics of United States immigration laws. Notwithstanding that U.S. citizens overwhelmingly oppose higher levels of alien entry and indeed support the lowering of levels, most Americans are unaware of existing policies which virtually welcome terrorists into the United States.

Incredibly, as the law now stands, membership in a terrorist organization and even advocacy of terrorist acts do not bar foreigners from entry into the United States or outright American citizenship. So an alien who is discovered to be currently belonging to a Middle Eastern terrorist organization, and who has publicly stated that the Empire State Building should be blown up, is not barred from entry to America or U.S. citizenship.

The law that permits this horror is the Immigration and Naturalization Act of 1990, sponsored by Senator Ted Kennedy. It instructs the State Department, which is responsible for screening these potential immigrants, that "mere" membership in terrorist organizations or even advocacy of mass murder should not exclude them from obtaining immigration visas.

What, pray tell, must they do to be prevented from entering, then? Well, it is left ultimately to the State Department screener to evaluate the "intent" of this potential American. In other words, merely harboring these views or belonging to a terrorist outfit or both cannot alone exclude an alien from entry. This person must be shown to possess the "intent" to blow up the Empire State Building. According to the State Department manual, immigration law requires that a foreigner be denied a visa if he has "indicated intention to cause death or serious bodily harm, and/or incited terrorist activity."

Well, thanks. It's reassuring to know the government will keep someone out who admits he's about to blow up a building tomorrow. But the same person can enter if, along with membership in a terrorist group, he simply opines that it would be a good thing if the building were blown up tomorrow.

The State Department defines "incitement" as "the making of utterances, written or oral, which are intended to arouse, urge, provoke, stir up, instigate, persuade, or move another person to commit an act of terrorism." But again, merely "advocating" terrorism or belonging to a terror group cannot be used as grounds for exclusion. The manual states, "Only statements that directly further or abet the commission of a terrorist act may properly constitute a basis for denying a visa."

Responding to an inquiry by James Barnett of the National Journalism Center, a State Department spokesman confirmed that a person who advocates terrorism but is not currently involved in an actual terrorist act is "not automatically ineligible for a visa."

The spokesman continued, "It has to do with intent... If I am a student in France, and I hate the United States and I'm sitting in my dorm room with five other people with me, and I say, 'We ought to blow up the U.S. embassy in Paris.' Is that actually intended? Do you think somebody would do it?"

Well, yes. But the spokesman was certainly giving an accurate representation of what the regulations state: "Statements approving a specific terrorist act, and asserting that such acts should be repeated, do not render an applicant ineligible."

Has America lost its mind? President Bush has repeatedly asserted the fierce resolve and determination of the American people and the federal government in the war on terrorism, which has been buttressed by his 92 percent approval rating. How about starting with a demand that this obscene law be repealed? It is beyond even the most juvenile comprehension that America should never allow an immigrant who advocates terrorism and belongs to a known terrorist organization.

In 1990, the same year the Kennedy law was enacted (signed

by Bush's father, by the way), the Egyptian sheik Omar Abdel-Rahman was admitted into the United States legally with a visa issued by the embassy in the Sudan. At the time, it was well-known that Abdel-Rahman's name appeared on a list of undesirables with terrorist links. Still, he was allowed to walk through. Abdel-Rahman, of course, was later convicted as a conspirator in the 1993 World Trade Center bombings, the trailblazer to the September 11 attacks. Today, he still sits in an American prison.

Kennedy explained his legislation at the time by stating, "The exclusion categories are reformed and updated to end outdated ideological, medical and communicable disease provisions." Oh, so this was about progress.

While American troops are currently bombing terrorists into the stone age half a world away in Afghanistan, the American government might consider some sensible action right here at home preventing mad bombers and other disciples of Satan from walking right through the border.

About the Author

Frank Borzellieri is a graduate of St. John's University, where he attended on a scholarship. He has worked as a journalist and editorialist and has been published in major publications such as *USA Today,* the *New York Daily News* and *Newsday.* He has been a columnist for the Ledger-Observer newspaper chain in New York City.

He is the author of "The Unspoken Truth: Race, Culture and Other Taboos" and the co-author of "It Happened in New York." He is currently working on two more books, the next of which is "Lynched: A Conservative's Life on a New York City School Board."

Mr. Borzellieri has been an elected member of School Board 24 in Queens, New York, where he has attained national stature for his stands in defense of a Eurocentric curriculum. He is best known for his opposition to multicultural and bilingual education. Because of his often one-man crusades on these issues, Mr. Borzellieri has come to be recognized as a national figure. He has appeared on ABC's "20/20" as an advocate for English as the official language.

He has also appeared on Fox Sunday Morning, Geraldo Rivera, Leeza Gibbons, Vladimir Posner, Ricki Lake, Michael Moore's "TV Nation" and many other television and radio programs as both guest and host. His radio appearances include Sean Hannity's program, as well as the top-rated programs of Bob Grant, Alan Colmes and Curtis Sliwa.

Frank Borzellieri has been profiled in the *New York Times*, the *Washington Times*, *Daily News*, *New York Post*, *Newsday*, *National Review*, the *Village Voice* and many others.